A Note From Rick Renner

I am on a personal quest to see a "revival of the Bible" so people can establish their lives on a firm foundation that will stand strong and endure the test when the end-time storm winds begin to intensify.

In order to experience a revival of the Bible in your personal life, it is important to take time each day to read, receive, and apply its truths to your life. James tells us that if we will continue in the perfect law of liberty — refusing to be forgetful hearers but determined to be doers — we will be blessed in our ways. As you watch or listen to the programs in this series and work through this corresponding study guide, I trust that you will search the Scriptures and allow the Holy Spirit to help you hear something new from God's Word that applies specifically to your life. I encourage you to be a doer of the Word that He reveals to you. Whatever the cost, I assure you — it will be worth it.

> Thy words were found, and I did eat them;
> and thy word was unto me the joy and rejoicing of mine heart:
> for I am called by thy name, O Lord God of hosts.
> — Jeremiah 15:16

Your brother and friend in Jesus Christ,

Rick Renner

Unless otherwise indicated, all scripture quotations are taken from the *King James Version* of the Bible.

Scripture quotations marked (*TLB*) are taken from *The Living Bible* copyright © 1971. Used by permission of Tyndale House Publishers, Inc., Carol Stream, Illinois 60188. All rights reserved.

You Are the Temple of the Holy Spirit

Copyright © 2020 by Rick Renner
8316 E. 73rd St.
Tulsa, Oklahoma 74133

Published by Rick Renner Ministries
www.renner.org

ISBN 13: 978-1-68031-814-2

eBook ISBN 13: 978-1-68031-815-9

All rights reserved. No portion of this book may be reproduced or transmitted in any form or by any means — electronic, mechanical, photocopy, recording, scanning, or other — except for brief quotations in critical reviews or articles, without the prior written permission of the Publisher.

How To Use This Study Guide

This ten-lesson study guide corresponds to *"You Are the Temple of the Holy Spirit" With Rick Renner* (Renner TV). Each lesson in this study guide covers a topic that is addressed during the program series, with questions and references supplied to draw you deeper into your own private study of the Scriptures on this subject.

To derive the most benefit from this study guide, consider the following:

First, watch or listen to the program prior to working through the corresponding lesson in this guide. (Programs can also be viewed at **renner.org** by clicking on the Media/Archives links.)

Second, take the time to look up the scriptures included in each lesson. Prayerfully consider their application to your own life.

Third, use a journal or notebook to make note of your answers to each lesson's Study Questions and Practical Application challenges.

Fourth, invest specific time in prayer and in the Word of God to consult with the Holy Spirit. Write down the scriptures or insights He reveals to you.

Finally, take action! Whatever the Lord tells you to do according to His Word, do it.

For added insights on this subject, it is recommended that you obtain Rick Renner's book *A Life Ablaze: Ten Simple Keys To Living on Fire for God*. You may also select from Rick's other available resources by placing your order at **renner.org** or by calling 1-800-742-5593.

LESSON 1

TOPIC
You Are God's Special Project

SCRIPTURES
1. **1 Corinthians 6:19** — What? know ye not that your body is the temple of the Holy Ghost which is in you, which ye have of God, and ye are not your own?
2. **John 1:12** — But as many as received him, to them gave he power to become the sons of God, even to them that believe on his name.
3. **Ephesians 2:1-5** — And you *hath he quickened*, who were dead in trespasses and sins; Wherein in time past ye walked according to the course of this world, according to the prince of the power of the air, the spirit that now worketh in the children of disobedience: Among whom also we all had our conversation in times past in the lusts of our flesh, fulfilling the desires of the flesh and of the mind; and were by nature the children of wrath, even as others. But God, who is rich in mercy, for his great love wherewith he loved us, Even when we were dead in sins, hath quickened us together with Christ, (by grace ye are saved).

GREEK WORDS
1. "temple" — ναός (*naos*): a temple or a highly decorated shrine; the image of vaulted ceilings, marble, granite, gold, silver, and highly decorated ornamentation; the most sacred, innermost part of a temple; the holy of holies
2. "dead" — νεκρός (*nekros*): a lifeless corpse; a cadaver with no life left in it
3. "in time past" — ἐν αἷς ποτε (*en hais pote*): back then
4. "according to" — κατά (*kata*): a downward force; domination or subjugation; controlled by
5. "course" — κόσμος (*kosmos*): conveys ideas of order and arrangement; describes society because it is a system that possesses order and arrangement; also carries with it the ideas of fashion and sophistication

6. "world" — **αἰῶνος** (*aionos*): an age with a concrete beginning and a concrete ending; a measurable and limited period of time, like a century or decade or generation
7. "the prince" — **τὸν ἄρχοντα** (*ton archonta*): from **ἄρχων** (*archon*) with a definite article; the prince, the ruler, the preeminent authority figure; the one with influence and jurisdiction in a particular realm
8. "worketh" — **ἐνεργοῦντος** (*energountos*): from **ἐνεργέω** (*energeo*), energy; a power that energizes or activates; depicts a powerful force that is set into motion; active power; here, an energizing presence
9. "disobedience" — **ἀπείθεια** (*apeitheia*): **πείθω** (*peitho*) and an **ἀ** (*a*) affixed to it; when transformed into **ἀπειθής** (*apeithes*), it means unpersuadable, uncontrollable, or unleadable; belligerent; non-compliant; obstinate; no longer able to persuade, control, lead, or exercise authority over; rebellious
10. "conversation" — **ἀναστρέφω** (*anastrepho*): lifestyle; portrays one's rising up and sitting down
11. "in times past" — **ποτε** (*pote*): at that time; back then
12. "lusts" — **ἐπιθυμία** (*epithumia*): from **ἐπί** (*epi*) and **θυμός** (*thumos*); the word **ἐπί** (*epi*) means over and gives intensity to the word; the word **θυμός** (*thumos*) is uncontrollable passion; passionate desire; in this verse, desire, cravings, carnal longings of the flesh; bent over and craving a thing
13. "by nature" — **φύσις** (*phusis*): nature; inherent nature; in-born instinct; by birth
14. "wrath" — **ὀργή** (*orge*): something so bent and twisted that it does not deserve to exist; something so warped that it must be destroyed
15. "but" — **δὲ** (*de*): an emphatic break in the text to emphasize the next statement
16. "rich" — **πλούσιος** (*plousios*): wealth so great it cannot be tabulated; abundant wealth; vast wealth; extreme riches; incredible abundance; magnificent opulence; extravagant lavishness; used by Plato to say no one was richer than legendary King Midas
17. "mercy" — **ἔλεος** (*eleos*): pity; compassion; a heart-wrenching emotion that compels one to action
18. "great" — **πολύς** (*polus*): a great numeric quantity; depicts something numerically enormous; incalculable

19. "love" — ἀγάπη (*agape*): a divine love that gives and gives, even if it's never responded to, thanked, or acknowledged; a love so profound that it knows no limits or boundaries in how far, wide, high, and deep it will go to show that love to its recipient; a sacrificial love that moves the lover to action
20. "grace" — χάρις (*charis*): a touch of the gods resulting in favor or grace; an empowering touch; an empowering presence, always demonstrating itself with a visible manifestation; a power that changes individuals; a power that enables one to do what he previously could not do or to be what he could never previously be
21. "saved" — σῴζω (*sodzo*): conveys the ideas of wholeness or salvation; wholeness in every part of life; a touch of salvation that brings delivering and healing power that results in wholeness; to deliver one's country from enemies; to protect, keep safe, to keep under protection

SYNOPSIS

The ten lessons in this study entitled *You Are the Temple of the Holy Spirit* will focus on the following topics:

- You Are God's Special Project
- You Are God's Masterpiece
- You Are Born by the Power of God
- You Are Sealed and Guaranteed by God's Spirit
- You Are a Repository of God's Greatest Treasure
- You Are a Brand-New Creature
- You Are the Corporate Temple of the Holy Spirit
- You Are Filled With the Riches of Christ
- You Are Called To Be a Saint
- You Are Represented by a Personal High Priest

The emphasis of this lesson:

Ultimately, Satan is the energizing presence that is dominating and controlling the world. Before we were saved, our lives were dominated and controlled by him and the whims of the world around us. We pursued the lusts of our flesh and wanted nothing to do with God. It was God who loved us and mercifully pursued us.

St. Isaac's Cathedral is located in Saint Petersburg, Russia, and its foundation was first laid in 1818 by Emperor Alexander I just after his victory over Napoleon. It took 40 years to construct this magnificent cathedral, which consists of more than 300,000 tons of materials. Workers used 20 different kinds of stone from Russia and all over Europe, including 16 tons of malachite and 1,100 pounds of deep blue lapis. The interior of this shrine was simply spectacular.

Yet, as beautiful as St. Isaac's Cathedral is, it pales in comparison to our inner beauty as the temple of the Holy Spirit! When we received Jesus as our Lord and Savior, the fullness of God moved into our lives, and we became His home. As a believer, you are a living, breathing sanctuary of the Spirit of God.

You Are God's Temple

In First Corinthians 6:19, the apostle Paul wrote, "What? know ye not that your body is the temple of the Holy Ghost which is in you, which ye have of God, and ye are not your own?" The word "temple" in this verse is the Greek word *naos*, and it describes *a temple* or *a highly decorated shrine*. It is the image of vaulted ceilings, marble, granite, gold, silver, and highly decorated ornamentation. This word can also refer to *the most sacred, innermost part of a temple; the holy of holies*.

Every person who confesses Jesus Christ is Lord becomes a temple of the Holy Spirit. God immediately moves inside and goes to work creating a pristine dwelling place for His Spirit. The Bible says, "But as many as received him, to them gave he power to become the sons of God, even to them that believe on his name" (John 1:12). God exerted great power within us in order to make us His sons and daughters.

The fact is, our lives were a complete mess before the grace of God touched us. The apostle Paul makes this clear in his letter to the Ephesians, saying, "And you *hath he quickened*, who were dead in trespasses and sins" (Ephesians 2:1). What's interesting is that the words "hath he quickened" do not appear in the original Greek text. They were supplied by the translators. In Greek, the verse simply says, "And you who were dead in trespasses and sins."

The word "dead" in this verse is the Greek word *nekros*, and it describes *a lifeless corpse* or *a cadaver with no life left in it*. Spiritually speaking, before salvation, we were like a lifeless corpse. We were not thinking about or looking for God. It was God that was in pursuit of us. As dead people, we simply did not have the ability to find God on our own. Jesus confirmed this in John 6:44, which says, "No man can come to me, except the Father which hath sent me draw him...."

Our Lives Were Once Dominated and Controlled by the World Around Us

The Bible goes on to say, "Wherein in time past ye walked according to the course of this world, according to the prince of the power of the air, the spirit that now worketh in the children of disobedience" (Ephesians 2:2). Notice the phrase "in time past." It is *en hais pote* in Greek, and it means *back then*. It is the equivalent of Paul saying, "Let's think back to what we were like *back then* when we were spiritually dead." It's almost as if Paul takes out his wallet and pulls out a picture of what we used to look like before we were saved by God's grace.

Paul said, "Back then you walked 'according to' the course of this world." The phrase "according to" is a translation of the Greek word *kata*, which describes *a downward force; domination* or *subjugation*. It can also mean *controlled*. Thus, before we were saved, our lives were *dominated, controlled,* and even *manipulated* by "the course of this world."

The word "course" is the Greek word *kosmos*, which conveys the idea of *order and arrangement*. It was used in the First Century to describe *society* because it is a system that possesses order and arrangement. The word *kosmos* could also be used to denote *fashion* and *sophistication*. Hence, before the grace of God touched our lives, we were dominated, manipulated, and controlled by society around us — by the news, by education, by entertainment, by fashionable trends, and even by the government.

This brings us to the word "world," which is actually a very poor translation. It is the Greek word *aionos*, and it describes *an age with a concrete beginning and a concrete ending*. It is *a measurable and limited period of time, like a century or decade or generation*. By using this word, Paul is telling us that those who are unsaved do not have an eternal perspective; they live by the fluctuating views or whims of the age in which they live. Whatever way the winds of society are blowing, that's the way they think.

Satan Is the Energizing Presence Dominating and Controlling Society

Then Paul pulled back the curtain and revealed the real dominating force working behind the scenes in society. He said those without Christ live "…according to the prince of the power of the air, the spirit that now worketh in the children of disobedience" (Ephesians 2:2). Again, we see the phrase "according to," which is a translation of the Greek word *kata*, indicating *a downward force that is dominating, subjugating* and *manipulating*.

The controlling force that is manipulating and dominating the unsaved is "the prince of the power of the air." This is Satan. In Greek, the phrase "the prince" is *ton archonta*, which is from the word *archon* but with a definite article. It describes *the prince, the ruler,* or *the preeminent authority figure; the one with influence and jurisdiction in a particular realm*. Satan does not have authority over the universe or over nature. But he does have authority in the realm of the world's system, working through people and the whims of the times. He uses things like governments, entertainment, and the court system to achieve his agenda.

As the prince of the power of the air, the devil is a spirit "…that now worketh in the children of disobedience" (Ephesians 2:2). The word "worketh" is the Greek word *energountos*, which is from the word *energeo*, and it describes *energy — a power that energizes or activates*. This word depicts *a powerful force that is set into motion; active power*. In this verse, it signifies *an energizing presence*. Hence, Satan is the energizing presence working in the children of disobedience.

The word "disobedience" is the Greek word *apeitheia*, which is the word *peitho* with an *a* affixed to it. When transformed into the word *apeithes*, it means *unpersuadable, uncontrollable, or unleadable*. It describes one who is *belligerent, non-compliant,* or *obstinate*. This person is *no longer able to persuade, control, lead, or exercise authority over*; they are *rebellious*. This is a clear picture of Satan's goal: to create a world system filled with people that are obstinate and rebellious to the principles and standards of God's Word.

Before We Were Saved We All Pursued the Passions of Our Flesh

When we come to Ephesians 2:3, Paul said, "Among whom also we all had our conversation in times past in the lusts of our flesh, fulfilling the desires of the flesh and of the mind; and were by nature the children of wrath, even as others." Here, he addresses all believers — including those of us who think we weren't so bad — and reminds us that at one time, all of us were a part of the disobedient crowd.

Paul said we had our "conversation in times past." The word "conversation" is the Greek word *anastrepho*, which describes *a lifestyle*. It portrays *one's rising up and sitting down, one's going in and going out*. Hence, "in times past" — which is the Greek word *pote*, meaning *at that time or back then* — when we were not saved, our entire life was dominated by the enemy who was working through the fleeting whims of society. We were dead in our sins and had no idea of eternal things. This is still the condition of the lost people in society today. In order for their eyes to be opened to the truth, it takes a real miracle of God.

Again, Paul said, "Among whom also we all had our conversation in times past in the lusts of our flesh, fulfilling the desires of the flesh and of the mind..." (Ephesians 2:3). The word "lusts" here is the Greek word *epithumia*. It is a compound of the word *epi*, which means *over* and gives intensity to the word; and the word *thumos*, which describes *uncontrollable passion* or *passionate desire*. When these words are compounded to form *epithumia*, it describes *desire, cravings, or carnal longings of the flesh*. It depicts *one bent over and craving a thing*.

No One Taught Us How To Sin
It Was Part of Our Nature

Paul went on to say that before we were saved, we "...were by nature the children of wrath, even as others" (Ephesians 2:3). The phrase "by nature" is the Greek word *phusis*, which describes *inherent nature* or *in-born instinct*. It is *something one knows by birth*. For instance, if you have ever seen baby fish birthed, you would notice that they immediately know how to swim. The mother fish does not take the time or effort to teach them; they already instinctively know how to swim. It's part of their nature.

The apostle Paul used this word *phusis* — translated here "by nature" — to describe our tendency to sin before we were saved. No one had to teach us how to lie, cheat, steal or do anything else that is wrong. Sinning came easy because it was a part of our nature. Through Adam, we acquired the sin genes and were by nature "children of wrath," which in Greek describes *something so bent and twisted that it does not deserve to exist; something so warped that it must be destroyed.*

Thank God He did not leave us in our helpless condition. The Bible says, "But God, who is rich in mercy, for his great love wherewith he loved us, even when we were dead in sins, hath quickened us together with Christ, (by grace ye are saved)" (Ephesians 2:4,5). Friend, God woke us up from our spiritual death and made us alive together with Christ. He gave us the faith to believe and receive Jesus as our Lord and Savior, and then He moved into our lives and made us His temple. We are His special project.

STUDY QUESTIONS

Study to shew thyself approved unto God, a workman that needeth not to be ashamed, rightly dividing the word of truth.
— 2 Timothy 2:15

1. First Corinthians 6:19 says, "…Your body is the temple of the Holy Ghost which is in you…." What is interesting is that this truth is repeated in First Corinthians 3:16 and Second Corinthians 6:16, and also mentioned in John 14:23; Romans 8:11; and Galatians 4:6. Why do you think God restates this so many times in His Word? What do these verses speak to you personally?
2. What does God say about all humanity in Romans 3:10-12, which is repeated in Psalm 14:1-3? In light of these verses and what Jesus said in John 6:44, if someone is asking questions about God and spiritual things, what can you know is happening in their life?

PRACTICAL APPLICATION

But be ye doers of the word, and not hearers only, deceiving your own selves.
— James 1:22

1. According to Ephesians 2:3, before we were saved, we were all a part of the disobedient crowd. Can you remember what your life was like before you surrendered to Jesus? What are some of the habits and hang-ups He set you free of?
2. What is the value of looking back and remembering what your life was like *before* you surrendered to Jesus? And why do you think it is

important to always remember Jesus' words in John 6:44: "No man can come to me, except the Father which hath sent me draw him…."?

LESSON 2

TOPIC
You Are God's Masterpiece

SCRIPTURES

1. **1 Corinthians 6:19** — What? know ye not that your body is the temple of the Holy Ghost which is in you, which ye have of God, and ye are not your own?
2. **Ephesians 1:13** — In whom ye also trusted, after that ye heard the word of truth, the gospel of your salvation: in whom also after that ye believed, ye were sealed with that holy Spirit of promise
3. **Ephesians 2:1-10** — And you *hath he quickened,* who were dead in trespasses and sins; Wherein in time past ye walked according to the course of this world, according to the prince of the power of the air, the spirit that now worketh in the children of disobedience: Among whom also we all had our conversation in times past in the lusts of our flesh, fulfilling the desires of the flesh and of the mind; and were by nature the children of wrath, even as others. But God, who is rich in mercy, for his great love wherewith he loved us, Even when we were dead in sins, hath quickened us together with Christ, (by grace ye are saved). And hath raised us up together, and made us sit together in heavenly places in Christ Jesus: That in the ages to come he might shew the exceeding riches of his grace in his kindness toward us through Christ Jesus. For by grace are ye saved through faith; and that not of yourselves: it is the gift of God: Not of works, lest any man should boast. For we are his workmanship, created in Christ Jesus unto good works, which God hath before ordained that we should walk in them.

GREEK WORDS

1. "temple" — ναός (*naos*): a temple or a highly decorated shrine; the image of vaulted ceilings, marble, granite, gold, silver, and highly dec-

orated ornamentation; the most sacred, innermost part of a temple; the holy of holies

2. "conversation" — ἀναστρέφω (*anastrepho*): lifestyle; portrays one's rising up and sitting down

3. "by nature" — φύσις (*phusis*): nature; inherent nature; in-born instinct; by birth

4. "wrath" — ὀργή (*orge*): something so bent and twisted that it does not deserve to exist; something so warped that it must be destroyed

5. "but" — δὲ (*de*): an emphatic break in the text to emphasize the next statement

6. "rich" — πλούσιος (*plousios*): wealth so great it cannot be tabulated; abundant wealth; vast wealth; extreme riches; incredible abundance; magnificent opulence; extravagant lavishness; used by Plato to say no one was richer than legendary King Midas

7. "mercy" — ἔλεος (*eleos*): pity; compassion; a heart-wrenching emotion that compels one to action

8. "for" — διά (*dia*): because; on account of; in response to

9. "great" — πολύς (*polus*): a great numeric quantity; depicts something numerically enormous; incalculable

10. "love" — ἀγάπη (*agape*): a divine love that gives and gives, even if it's never responded to, thanked, or acknowledged; a love so profound that it knows no limits or boundaries in how far, wide, high, and deep it will go to show that love to its recipient; a sacrificial love that moves the lover to action

11. "dead" — νεκρός (*nekros*): a lifeless corpse; a cadaver with no life left in it

12. "shew" — ἐνδείκνυμι (*endeiknumi*): to show off; to demonstrate; to make fully evident; to openly display

13. "exceeding" — ὑπερβάλλω (*huperballo*): something that is above and beyond what is normal; exceeding or surpassing; pictures an archer who aims his arrow at the bull's-eye, but shoots way over the top; depicts something beyond the range of anything considered normal; something unparalleled

14. "riches" — πλούσιος (*plousios*): wealth so great it cannot be tabulated; abundant wealth; vast wealth; extreme riches; incredible abundance; magnificent opulence; extravagant lavishness; used by Plato to say no one was richer than legendary King Midas

15. "kindness" — χρηστότης (*chrestotes*): kindness; benevolence
16. "workmanship" — ποίημα (*poiema*): poem; product; a thing made; workmanship
17. "created" — κτίζω (*ktidzo*): creation of something from nothing; not renewed or refashioned with old material, but brand-spanking new and never existing before; not enhanced, improved, repaired, or restored; something newly created and original

SYNOPSIS

For nearly half a century, St. Isaac's Cathedral in Saint Petersburg, Russia, was the central place of worship for the Russian Empire. Having 116,000 square feet, it could accommodate 14,000 people, and its interiors were absolutely magnificent.

This cathedral is built of more than 300,000 tons of materials, including 16 tons of malachite and 1,100 pounds of deep blue lapis. There are also 20 different kinds of marble from all over Russia and Europe, and more than 881 pounds of gold used in its ornamentations and decorations.

As beautiful as the interiors of St. Isaac's are, they pale in comparison to our spiritual interiors. What God did in us at the moment of our birth into His family was wonderful beyond words. The Bible says, "…After that ye heard the word of truth, the gospel of your salvation: in whom also after that ye believed, ye were sealed with that holy Spirit of promise" (Ephesians 1:13). This was God's way of saying, "What I've done in you is so amazing, I'm going to place My personal seal of approval on you and make you the home of My Spirit."

The emphasis of this lesson:

You are God's masterpiece. Out of the surpassing abundance of His grace, God put forth His most powerful and creative effort to make you brand-spanking new in Christ Jesus the day you got saved. He woke you up out of spiritual death and quickened you with Christ, turning you into something spectacular.

Our Condition Before Coming to Christ Was Deplorable

In Lesson 1, we saw that the apostle Paul wrote about our condition before coming to Christ and how utterly impossible it was for any of us to get saved. If God Himself had not started the process to bring us to Christ, none of us would have been saved. This is why Jesus said in John 6:44, "No man can come to me, except the Father which hath sent me draw him…." Thus, it is a supernatural work of God for a person to get saved.

Ephesians 2:1 says, "And you *hath he quickened*, who were dead in trespasses and sins." As we noted before, if you are reading from the *King James Version*, the words "hath he quickened" are italicized, which means they were supplied by the translators and are not in the original Greek text. The Greek simply says, "And you who were dead in trespasses and sins." This verse very abruptly and candidly describes our condition: we were dead spiritually.

Just like a lifeless corpse lying in a casket has no ability to respond, before we were saved, we were dead in sin and unable to find God. We had no desire for God, and nothing in us responded to Him, which is why salvation is such a miracle. It occurs because God comes to us — not because we go to God. It is the work of His grace that wakes us up spiritually and brings us to Christ.

The Bible goes on to say, "Wherein in time past ye walked according to the course of this world, according to the prince of the power of the air, the spirit that now worketh in the children of disobedience: among whom also we all had our conversation in times past in the lusts of our flesh, fulfilling the desires of the flesh and of the mind; and were by nature the children of wrath, even as others" (Ephesians 2:2,3).

This passage lets us know clearly that all of us were once under the dominating and controlling influence of Satan. So regardless of how good any of us think we may have been, the Bible says we were all dominated and manipulated by the lusts of our flesh. Moreover, it says we were, "…by nature the children of wrath, even as others" (Ephesians 2:3). The phrase "by nature" is the Greek word *phusis*, which describes *nature, inherent nature,* or *in-born instinct.* It is *something you received by birth.*

Just as newborn guppies don't need any swimming lessons because they instinctively know how to swim from birth, we don't need anyone to teach us how to sin. The moment we were born, we inherently knew how to sin; it was a part of our fallen nature we inherited from Adam. As a result, the Bible says we were children of "wrath," which is the Greek word *orge*, and it describes *something so bent and twisted that it does not deserve to exist. It is something so warped that it must be destroyed.* That is the condition of mankind without God — he is unable to fix or reform himself. In fact, we are so twisted and warped that we don't even deserve to live.

But God got involved!

God Is Rich in Mercy and Love

Ephesians 2:4 says, "But God, who is rich in mercy, for his great love wherewith he loved us." Notice the word "but" that opens this verse. It is the Greek word *de*, which is *an emphatic break in the text to emphasize the next statement.* Paul had just spent the first three verses of Ephesians 2 describing our condition when we were lost and dead in our sins. This word *de* — translated here as "but" — is a dramatic pause to let everyone know that what they are about to hear is really great news.

The Bible says, "But God, who is rich in mercy..." (Ephesians 2:4). The word "rich" here is the Greek word *plousios*, and it describes *wealth so great it cannot be tabulated.* It is *abundant wealth; vast wealth; extreme riches; incredible abundance; magnificent opulence; and extravagant lavishness.* The word *plousios* was used by Plato to say no one was richer than legendary King Midas, and now this word is being used by Paul to describe the immeasurable mercy of God. One expositor of Scripture has said this means *God is filthy, stinking rich* when it comes to the commodity of mercy.

The word "mercy" is the Greek word *eleos*, which can be translated as *pity* or *compassion*. In this case, it depicts *a heart-wrenching emotion that compels one to action.* This helps us understand and better appreciate Jesus' words in John 3:16: "For God so loved the world, that he gave his only begotten Son, that whosoever believeth in him should not perish, but have everlasting life."

Aren't you grateful that God didn't just look at us and wring his hands and say, "Oh, they're such a mess! They are so flawed, so defective, so warped, so bent, so twisted, and so dead in sin. What am I going to do about them?" Instead, He was moved to action. That is what mercy does, and that is what we see taking place in Ephesians 2:4. Basically, God said, "I love them so much I have to do something about their condition." Then out of His great, abundant wealth of mercy, He was moved to send Jesus into the world to do what we could never do by ourselves.

Again, the Scripture says, "But God, who is rich in mercy, for his great love wherewith he loved us" (Ephesians 2:4). The word "for" in this verse is the Greek word *dia*, which actually means *because*; *on account of*; or *in response to*. The word "great" in Greek is *polus*, and it describes *a great numeric quantity*. It depicts *something numerically enormous* or *incalculable*.

This brings us to the word "love," which is the wonderful Greek word *agape*. This word depicts *a divine love that gives and gives, even if it's never responded to, thanked, or acknowledged*. God is the initiator of *agape* love — *a love so profound that it knows no limits or boundaries in how far, wide, high, and deep it will go to show that love to its recipient*. It is *a sacrificial love that moves the lover to action*.

With this understanding, we could translate Ephesians 2:4, "But God, who is filthy stinking rich when it comes to how much mercy He has, was moved to action in order to satisfy His incalculable profound love that He has for us."

God's Grace and Kindness Are Immeasurably Beyond One's Imagination

When we come to Ephesians 2:5, we see Paul once again describing our appalling, pre-salvation condition — this time in sharp contrast to God's saving grace. He said, "Even when we were dead in sins, [God] hath quickened us together with Christ, (by grace ye are saved). The word "dead" here is again the Greek word *nekros*, which describes *a lifeless corpse*; *a cadaver with no life left in it*. So while we were spiritually dead and unable to do anything to change or better ourselves, God initiated His plan of salvation, and it was totally a result of His grace.

Paul went on to say, "And [God] hath raised us up together, and made us sit together in heavenly places in Christ Jesus: that in the ages to come he might shew the exceeding riches of his grace in his kindness toward us through Christ Jesus" (Ephesians 2:6,7). The word "riches" in this verse is again the Greek word *plousios*, which describes *wealth so great it cannot be tabulated*. It is *abundant wealth*; *vast wealth*; *extreme riches*; *incredible abundance*; *magnificent opulence*; or *extravagant lavishness*. And the word "kindness" is the Greek word *chrestotes*, which means *benevolence*.

Now in front of the phrase "riches of his grace in his kindness" is the word "exceeding," which is the Greek word *huperballo*. It is a compound of the word *huper*, which describes *something excessive or beyond*, and the word *ballo*, which means *to throw something* like throwing a ball or a rock. When these words are compounded to form *huperballo*, it depicts *something that is above and beyond what is normal; something exceeding or surpassing*. It pictures an archer who aims his arrow at the bullseye, but shoots way over the top of the target. Furthermore, it depicts *something beyond the range of anything considered normal; something unparalleled*.

The Bible says God saved us so "that in the ages to come he might shew the exceeding riches of his grace in his kindness toward us through Christ Jesus" (Ephesians 2:7). The word "shew" in this passage means *to show off; to demonstrate; to make fully evident*; or *to openly display*. The use of this word and the word *huperballo* — translated here "exceeding" — is the equivalent of God saying, "I'm really going to show off my goodness and kindness in the lives of humanity. While they're still spiritually dead, I'm going to wake them up and make them totally new in Christ. This will really demonstrate the unparalleled riches of My grace and My benevolence."

You Are God's Masterpiece!

After Paul explained the abundant kindness and goodness of God in light of our helpless condition, he wrote two very powerful verses concerning our salvation. "For by grace are ye saved through faith; and that not of yourselves: it is the gift of God: not of works, lest any man should boast" (Ephesians 2:8,9). So from the beginning to the end, our salvation is a complete work of grace. God initiated the work and brought it into being on His own — with no assistance from us.

To this Paul added, "For we are his workmanship, created in Christ Jesus unto good works, which God hath before ordained that we should walk in them" (Ephesians 2:10). The word "workmanship" is the Greek word *poiema*, and it describes *a poem*; *a product*; or *a thing made*. It is actually the word for *a masterpiece*.

The word *poiema* carries the idea of *something that is artfully created*. It denotes *one who has the ability to write or create a literary masterpiece*. Paul used the word *poiema* to explain what happened when you became a child of God, and it emphatically means that on the day you got saved, God put forth His most powerful and creative effort to make you new. Once God was finished making you new, you became *a masterpiece*, skillfully and artfully created in Christ Jesus. Hence, God's creative, artistic, intelligent genius went into your making.

Also notice it says you were "created in Christ Jesus." The word "created" is the Greek word *ktidzo*, and it describes *the creation of something from nothing*. This is not something renewed or refashioned with old material, but brand-spanking new and never existing before. It is not something enhanced, improved, repaired, or restored. It is *something newly created and original*.

Wow! Look how much you've been given in Jesus Christ! When you were spiritually dead, God woke you up and quickened you with Christ and turned you into something spectacular. You are His workmanship — which means you are God's masterpiece! What He did in you far surpasses anything anyone could have imagined. In His unsurpassing kindness and benevolence, He made you brand-spanking new. You are a trophy of His grace, and according to First Corinthians 6:19, "…Your body is the temple of the Holy Ghost which is in you.…"

STUDY QUESTIONS

Study to shew thyself approved unto God, a workman that needeth not to be ashamed, rightly dividing the word of truth.
— 2 Timothy 2:15

The enemy loves to remind you of who you used to be and all that you used to do wrong. But now that you are a believer in Christ, *everything has changed*! The way God sees you is the way *you* need to see yourself. To help you solidify your new identity in Christ, look up these verses and write a personal declaration of what they say about you. The first one is done for you.

- 1 Corinthians 3:16 – *"I am the temple of God, and His Spirit lives in me."*
- 2 Corinthians 5:17 – _____
- 2 Corinthians 5:21 – _____
- Ephesians 1:6 – _____

- Ephesians 1:7 – _____
- Ephesians 2:6 – _____
- Ephesians 2:10 – _____
- 1 John 3:1,2 – _____

PRACTICAL APPLICATION

> But be ye doers of the word, and not hearers only,
> deceiving your own selves.
> —James 1:22

1. Have you ever stopped to think about the fact that no one had to teach you how to sin? Lying, cheating, and being selfish all came naturally. What does that say to you personally about your condition apart from God? How does it change the way you see your children and grandchildren and your responsibility in their lives?
2. With the realization of just how dead you were before surrendering your life to Christ — and how powerless you were to do anything about it — carefully reread Ephesians 2:8 and 9. How is your perception of this passage and God's saving grace different now?

LESSON 3

TOPIC

You Are Born by the Power of God

SCRIPTURES

1. **1 Corinthians 6:19** — What? know ye not that your body is the temple of the Holy Ghost which is in you, which ye have of God, and ye are not your own?
2. **2 Corinthians 5:17** — Therefore if any man be in Christ, he is a new creature: old things are passed away; behold, all things are become new.
3. **John 1:12,13** — But as many as received him, to them gave he power to become the sons of God, even to them that believe on his name.

Which were born, not of blood, nor of the will of the flesh, nor of the will of man, but of God.

4. **2 Corinthians 4:4** — In whom the god of this world hath blinded the minds of them which believe not, lest the light of the glorious gospel of Christ, who is the image of God, should shine unto them.

GREEK WORDS

1. "temple" — ναός (*naos*): a temple or a highly decorated shrine; the image of vaulted ceilings, marble, granite, gold, silver, and highly decorated ornamentation; the most sacred, innermost part of a temple; the holy of holies
2. "as many" — ὅσος (*hosos*): as many as; as great as; as much as; an unlimited number
3. "received" — λαμβάνω (*lambano*): to seize or to lay hold of something in order to make it your very own, almost like a person who reaches out to grab, to capture, or to take possession of something; in some cases, it means to violently lay hold of something in order to seize and take it as one's very own; at other times it depicts one who graciously receives something that is freely and easily given
4. "gave" — δίδωμι (*didomi*): to give; to bestow as a gift; to give to one asking; to supply; to furnish; to give into one's care; to entrust; to commit
5. "power" — ἐξουσία (*exousia*): delegated authority, influence; denotes one who has received delegated power; the legal right
6. "become" — γίνομαι (*ginomai*): to suddenly become; to transition from one thing to another
7. "believe" — πιστεύω (*pisteuo*): to persuade, to trust, to believe; a persuasion from God imparts an impulse or "divine spark" to believe
8. "on" — εἰς (*eis*): into
9. "name" — ὄνομα (*onoma*): name; it denotes a person's character and reputation that distinguishes him from others
10. "blinded" — τυφλόω (*tuphloo*): blind; doesn't just depict a person who is unable to see, but a person who has been intentionally blinded by someone else; one whose eyes have been deliberately removed so that he is blinded; this individual hasn't just lost his sight, he has no eyes to see

SYNOPSIS

As we have seen, St. Isaac's Cathedral in Saint Petersburg, Russia, is simply magnificent in beauty, and it served as the central cathedral for the entire Russian Empire for nearly half a century. The columns that adorn the altar inside this church is made up of 16 tons of malachite that artists painstakingly arranged piece by tiny piece to form a marvelous mosaic. There are also 1,100 pounds of deep blue lapis used in the decorations of this altar, all of which came from the land of Afghanistan.

Overall, St. Isaac's Cathedral is constructed of more than 300,000 tons of materials, including 20 different kinds of precious marble from all over the world and 155 massive paintings. Yet, even with all of its breathtaking beauty, it pales in comparison to the spiritual temple that God has crafted inside of us.

The moment we surrendered our lives to Christ, God immediately went to work inside of us, making us totally new. Rather than just repair us or make us into an improved version of what we were, He released His full power within us and recreated us into a masterpiece for His glory. You have been uniquely remade by the power of God and are a living, breathing habitation of His Holy Spirit!

The emphasis of this lesson:

Before you came to Christ, you were spiritually dead and totally powerless to change your condition. It was God who gave you the eyes to see your true spiritual state and your need for Jesus. He is also the One who gave you the power to believe on the name of Jesus and become a child of God. Your salvation is truly a miracle!

You Are a Divine Container of God's Spirit

In the two previous lessons, we have seen that our lives were a complete mess before the grace of God found us and saved us. We were dead in sin and dominated by the power of Satan, who is working through the world system and in the children of disobedience. "But God, who is rich in mercy, for his great love wherewith he loved us, even when we were dead in sin, hath quickened us together with Christ, (by grace ye are saved)" (Ephesians 2:4,5).

Friend, you are God's special project, and He turned you into a masterpiece. Now you are His forever home! First Corinthians 6:19 says, "What? know ye not that your body is the temple of the Holy Ghost which is in you, which ye have of God, and ye are not your own?"

In the *King James Version*, this verse begins with the word "what," which in Greek is an exclamation. The word "know" is a form of the Greek word *oida*, which means *to comprehend* or *to perceive*. And the word "not" is *the emphatic form of the word no*. Taken together, it is as if Paul is saying, "What! Do you not realize it? Do you not know and do you not comprehend, that your body is the temple of the Holy Ghost? Have you not gotten it yet? How could you possibly not understand that your body is God's temple?"

The word "body" is the Greek word *soma*, which is the word for the *physical body*. Paul told the Corinthian believers — and us — that our physical body is the temple of the Holy Spirit. The word "temple" here is the Greek word *naos*, which is the term for *a temple* or *a highly decorated shrine*. It depicts the image of vaulted ceilings, marble, granite, gold, silver, and highly decorated ornamentation. It is the same word used in the Old Testament Septuagint to describe *the most sacred, innermost part of a temple; the holy of holies*. Any Greek reader would have understood the meaning of the word *naos* because their cities had many temples that were highly decorated shrines.

Remember, you were initially spiritually dead in sin, but God in His abundant grace and benevolence woke you up and quickened you together with Christ, making you a walking sanctuary for His Spirit. Your body became a highly decorated shrine — a holy of holies — for the Holy Spirit to live in. First Corinthians 6:19 says, "…Your body is the temple of the Holy Ghost which is in you, which ye have of God…." The phrase "which ye have" is a form of the Greek word *echo*, which means *to hold, to have*, or *to possess*. The use of this word depicts our bodies as *divine containers* of the Spirit of Almighty God. It also helps us see why Paul said, "Therefore if any man be in Christ, he is a new creature: old things are passed away; behold, all things are become new" (2 Corinthians 5:17).

God Gave Us Power To Become His Sons and Daughters

Turning our attention once more to John 1:12, it says, "But as many as received him, to them gave he power to become the sons of God, even to them that believe on his name." Notice how this verse opens with the words "as many." In Greek, this is the word *hosos*, which means *as many as; as great as;* or *as much as*. It describes *an unlimited number*. This means in His kindness, God has thrown open the door to enter His family to anyone who will receive and believe in Jesus.

The word "received" in this verse is a form of the Greek word *lambano*, which means *to seize or to lay hold of something in order to make it your very own, almost like a person who reaches out to grab, to capture, or to take possession of something*. In some cases, the word *lambano* means *to violently lay hold of something in order to seize and take it as one's very own*. At other times, it depicts *one who graciously receives something that is freely and easily given*. The fact is, God offers everyone the gift of salvation, but we have to reach out and lay hold of it and seize it by faith.

Again, John 1:12 says, "But as many as received him, to them gave he power to become the sons of God...." The word "gave" here is a form of the Greek word *didomi*, which means *to give; to bestow as a gift; to give to one asking*. Moreover, it also means *to supply; to furnish; to give into one's care; to entrust;* or *to commit*. God entrusted and amply supplied us with the power we need to become His sons and daughters.

The word "power" is a form of the Greek word *exousia*, which describes *delegated authority* or *influence*. It denotes *one who has received delegated power* or *the legal right*. The reason God gave us the power or legal right to become His sons and daughters is because on our own, we didn't have the ability. Remember, we were dead in sin and unable to do anything to save ourselves. God initiated the restoration of our relationship with Him. Salvation is a gift from Him from start to finish.

Even the Ability To Believe Is a Gift From God

It is God Himself who gives us the power to become the sons of God. The word "become" is a form of the Greek word *ginomai*, which means *to suddenly become*. It describes *a transition from one thing to another*. In this case, it is describing the sudden transition from being spiritually dead to becoming spiritually alive in Christ.

Who is given this delegated authority to become God's children? It is those who "…believe on his name…" (John 1:12). The word "believe" is the Greek word *pisteuo*, and it means *to persuade, to trust,* or *to believe.* It is *a persuasion from God that imparts an impulse or "divine spark" to believe.* Therefore, if God did not give you the ability to believe, you would not be able to. Even the ability to believe is a gift from Him.

The Bible says this divine spark is given to believe "on His name." The word "on" is the Greek word *eis*, which means *into*, and it carries the idea of a *merger*. It depicts you entering into union with Jesus Himself. The word "name" is the Greek word *onoma*, which in addition to meaning *name* also denotes *a person's character and reputation that distinguishes him from others.* Hence, when you release your faith and believe on the name of Jesus, you enter into union with the very character of Jesus; a merger takes place and you become one with Him.

Are you seeing what a wonderful work of grace your salvation is? It is such a miracle that you could never produce it on your own. The Holy Spirit draws you to God, and God wakes you up from spiritual death and gives you the divine ability to believe and receive Jesus as your Lord and Savior. Indeed, "For by grace are ye saved through faith; and that not of yourselves: it is the gift of God: not of works, lest any man should boast" (Ephesians 2:8,9).

It Was God's Will For You To Be His Child

After talking about the gift of God's power and the ability to believe in Jesus, the apostle John went on to say, "[We] were born, not of blood, nor of the will of the flesh, nor of the will of man, but of God" (John 1:13). This verse clearly lets us know that our birth into God's family was not an accident nor was it the result of our human will or anyone else's will. When we became God's sons and daughters it was by God's will — period.

Friend, God wanted you — yes, *you* — as His child! It is He who gave you the "power," the *delegated authority* (*exousia*) to become His son or daughter the day you chose to make Jesus your Lord and Savior. Think of it — at that moment of decision, all the power and authority resident within the mighty name of Jesus Christ came to live on the inside of you! So, rather than complain that you're weak and nothing special, it's time to start laying claim to what is stored up inside you! The same explosive, dynamic, phenomenal authority and power that resides within Jesus has now been delegated to reside in *you*.

Salvation Is Truly a Miracle!

In Second Corinthians 4:4, the apostle Paul took time to explain why unbelievers do not understand the message of the Gospel. He said, "…The god of this world hath blinded the minds of them which believe not, lest the light of the glorious gospel of Christ, who is the image of God, should shine unto them."

The key word to understand in this verse is the word "blinded." It is a translation of the Greek word *tuphloo*, which doesn't just depict a person who is unable to see, but *a person who has been intentionally blinded by someone else*. It describes *one whose eyes have been deliberately removed so that he is blinded*. This individual hasn't just lost his sight — *he has no eyes to see*.

This is the condition you were in before you got saved. You were spiritually blinded by Satan, the god of this world. It is the same condition millions upon millions of other people are in at this very moment. Satan has blinded them; he's removed their eyes and they don't have the ability to see that they are spiritually dead. It is the Holy Spirit who gives those who are lost spiritual eyes to see their true spiritual condition and their desperate need for Jesus. And He gives them those eyes when the Gospel is presented to them.

When the Gospel is shared, the Holy Spirit begins to create spiritual eyes and spiritual ears in unbelievers, enabling them to see and hear and understand the truth. But this supernatural activity only takes place when the Gospel is shared. If unbelievers never hear the Good News, they'll never have eyes to see or ears to hear and understand the truth. That's why you need to share the Gospel.

Friend, as a believer in Christ, the Bible says, "…Your body is the temple of the Holy Ghost which is in you, which ye have of God, and ye are not your own" (1 Corinthians 6:19). You are a walking, breathing sanctuary of God. Through the surpassing riches of His grace and His benevolence, He has given you spiritual eyes to see. He has quickened you with Christ and given you the ability to believe on His Name and the delegated authority to become a child of God.

In our next lesson, you are going to see how when you got saved, God did something so miraculous inside of you that He placed His seal of approval on you. And that seal is none other than the Holy Spirit!

STUDY QUESTIONS

> Study to shew thyself approved unto God, a workman that needeth not to be ashamed, rightly dividing the word of truth.
> — 2 Timothy 2:15

1. Just how powerful is the "name of Jesus"? Take a few moments to look up these Bible verses and see for yourself!
   - Philippians 2:9-11
   - John 14:13,14
   - Acts 3:6,16
   - Proverbs 18:10
   - Malachi 1:11
   - Psalm 113:1-3
2. Friend, all the power and authority resident within the mighty name of Jesus Christ came to live on the inside of you the moment you were saved! Instead of complaining that you're weak and nothing special, begin laying claim to what is stored up inside you!

PRACTICAL APPLICATION

> But be ye doers of the word, and not hearers only, deceiving your own selves.
> — James 1:22

1. Second Corinthians 4:4 says that Satan, "…The god of this world hath blinded the minds of them which believe not…." Who do you know and love that is an unbeliever? What encouraging words does God speak about them in First Timothy 2:4?
2. Think for a moment. Have you ever shared the Gospel with these people? If so, when and how did they respond? If not, take time now

to pray for these individuals, asking God to remove their blindness and give them eyes to see their true spiritual condition and the ability to believe in and receive Jesus as Lord and Savior.

LESSON 4

TOPIC

You Are Sealed and Guaranteed by God's Spirit

SCRIPTURES

1. **1 Corinthians 6:19** — What? know ye not that your body is the temple of the Holy Ghost which is in you, which ye have of God, and ye are not your own?

2. **John 20:19-22** — Then the same day at evening, being the first day of the week, when the doors were shut where the disciples were assembled for fear of the Jews, came Jesus and stood in the midst, and saith unto them, Peace be unto you. And when he had so said, he shewed unto them his hands and his side. Then were the disciples glad, when they saw the Lord. Then said Jesus to them again, Peace be unto you: as my Father hath sent me, even so send I you. And when he had said this, he breathed on them, and saith unto them, Receive ye the Holy Ghost.

3. **Genesis 2:7** — And the Lord God formed man of the dust of the ground, and breathed into his nostrils the breath of life; and man became a living soul.

4. **Ephesians 1:13,14** — In whom ye also trusted, after that ye heard the word of truth, the gospel of your salvation: in whom also after that ye believed, ye were sealed with that holy Spirit of promise. Which is the earnest of our inheritance until the redemption of the purchased possession, unto the praise of his glory.

5. **2 Corinthian 1:22** — Who hath also sealed us, and given the earnest of the Spirit in our hearts.

GREEK WORDS
1. "temple" — ναός (*naos*): a temple or a highly decorated shrine; the image of vaulted ceilings, marble, granite, gold, silver, and highly decorated ornamentation; the most sacred, innermost part of a temple; the holy of holies
2. "breathed on them" — ἐμφυσάω (*emphusao*) to breathe into; to inflate
3. "receive" — Λάβετε (*labete*): to take right now; to actively receive
4. "believed" — πιστεύω (*pisteuo*): to persuade, to trust, to believe; a persuasion from God that imparts an impulse or "divine spark" to believe
5. "sealed" — σφραγίζω (*sphragidzo*): pictures a seal placed on a package after the product had been thoroughly examined and inspected to make sure it was fully intact and complete; the seal was proof the product was impeccable; normally such seals bore the insignia of a wealthy or famous person, which meant that this package was to be treated with tender care; the seal affirmed who was the owner and guaranteed the package would make it to its final destination
6. "earnest" — ἀρραβὼν (*arrabon*): a payment given in advance to guarantee the whole amount will be paid afterward; earnest-money; an installment; a deposit; a down-payment which guarantees full delivery of a promise; security deposit given by the purchaser to assure confidence and peace to the seller that he will fulfill his promise

SYNOPSIS
In the city of Saint Petersburg, Russia, there stands another magnificent towering cathedral — it is the Peter and Paul Cathedral. It is the first and oldest landmark in Saint Petersburg and was built under the direction of Peter the Great between 1712 and 1733 near the Neva River. It is truly a place of marvelous workmanship that is both elaborate and intricate. It boasts of one of the tallest church bell towers in the world, and its interiors are embellished with more than 22 pounds of gold. But as beautiful as this cathedral is, it pales in comparison to the outstanding work God has done inside of you.

The Bible tells us in Ephesians 2:10, "For we are his workmanship, created in Christ Jesus unto good works, which God hath before ordained that we should walk in them." When you were born again, God released His full power within you, making you a masterpiece of His own design. Spiritually speaking, your interiors are more magnificent than any cathedral in the world, and God's Spirit is living in you! You are the temple of the Holy Spirit!

The emphasis of this lesson:
The moment you were saved, God sealed you with the Holy Spirit, and that seal is His approval that He has thoroughly examined you and found nothing flawed or inferior in you. The Holy Spirit also serves as the earnest of your inheritance, which means He is the deposit or down-payment guaranteeing that God will fulfill His promises to you.

A Quick Review of Our Anchor Verse

In First Corinthians 6:19, our anchor verse, the apostle Paul wrote to the Corinthian believers — *and us* — and said, "What? know ye not that your body is the temple of the Holy Ghost which is in you, which ye have of God, and ye are not your own?"

We have seen that the word "temple" is the Greek word *naos*, which describes *a temple or a highly decorated shrine*. It is the image of vaulted ceilings, marble, granite, gold, silver, and highly decorated ornamentation. In fact, it is the exact same word used in the Old Testament Septuagint to describe *the most sacred, innermost part of a temple in Jerusalem; the holy of holies*. The use of this word *naos* tells us that when we got saved, God fashioned our human bodies to become the holy of holies for His Spirit. He no longer lives in physical buildings; He lives inside of us!

The Bible says your physical body has become the temple of the Holy Spirit "…which is in you, which ye have of God…" (1 Corinthians 6:19). The phrase "which ye have" is a form of the Greek word *echo*, which means *to hold, to have*, or *to possess*. The use of this word here depicts your body as a *divine container* of the Spirit of Almighty God. It took God's divine power to transform you into God's temple, and it is by that same divine power that you were sealed by the Holy Spirit unto the day of your redemption.

The Disciples Were the First To Become the Temple of the Holy Spirit

Just after Jesus was resurrected from the grave, He appeared to His disciples who were hiding in the Upper Room behind closed doors. The apostle

John presents the details of what took place, saying, "Then the same day at evening, being the first day of the week, when the doors were shut where the disciples were assembled for fear of the Jews, came Jesus and stood in the midst, and saith unto them, Peace be unto you" (John 20:19).

The first words Jesus spoke to the disciples when He saw them were, "Peace be unto you." He knew that He was about to birth them into the family of God, and they needed to be at peace in order to receive the gift He was about to give them. The Bible then says, "And when he had so said, he shewed unto them his hands and his side. Then were the disciples glad, when they saw the Lord. Then said Jesus to them again, Peace be unto you: as my Father hath sent me, even so send I you" (John 20:20,21).

Again, for a second time, Jesus spoke to His disciples and said, "Peace be unto you." This is important to note, because peace is the primary fruit of salvation. The Bible says, "And when he had said this, he breathed on them, and saith unto them, Receive ye the Holy Ghost" (John 20:22). This was the moment in time when the disciples were born again under the condition of the New Testament Covenant.

When the Bible says that Jesus "breathed on them," it uses the word *emphusao*, which means *to breathe into* or *to inflate*. It is the word one would use to describe breathing into a balloon to inflate it with air. In that moment, Jesus literally *breathed into* His disciples, and they received the breath of His Spirit.

What is interesting is that the word *emphusao* is the same word used in Genesis 2:7, which says, "And the Lord God formed man of the dust of the ground, and breathed into his nostrils the breath of life; and man became a living soul." The phrase "breathed into" is the word *emphusao* in the Greek Septuagint. It means God breathed into Adam and inflated his lungs, and in that very moment he became a living soul.

When Jesus "breathed into" His disciples, the Bible says He told them to "receive" the Holy Spirit. The word "receive" is the Greek word *labete*, which means *to take right now* or *to actively receive in this very moment*. Although some people have taught that Jesus was prophesying about the Holy Spirit coming on the Day of Pentecost, that is not true, and this word *labete* makes that clear. When Jesus breathed on them, He said, "Receive (*labete*) — take it right now; actively receive in this moment — the Holy Spirit."

Up until this point, the Holy Spirit had been on them and with them. But the Spirit had not taken up permanent residence *inside* of them. It was the same way for all of God's people in the Old Testament. The Holy Spirit would come upon them for a certain task or occupation. For example, the Spirit came upon Samson to fight the Philistines. Likewise, the Spirit came upon David to serve as king over the people of Israel.

This moment in John 20:22 was truly historic. It was the very first time ever that the Holy Spirit moved into the hearts of human beings, and they became the temple of God.

You Were 'Sealed' With the Holy Spirit

In Ephesians 1:13, the apostle Paul wrote about what happens when the Holy Spirit first enters a person's life at salvation. He said, "In whom ye also trusted, after that ye heard the word of truth, the gospel of your salvation: in whom also after that ye believed, ye were sealed with that holy Spirit of promise."

Notice it says "after that ye believed." In Greek, the word "believed" is *pisteuo*, and it means *to persuade, to trust,* or *to believe*. It is *a persuasion from God that imparts an impulse or "divine spark" to believe*. This again clearly shows us that the ability to believe in Christ comes from God Himself. Hence, our salvation from beginning to end is a result of God's marvelous grace. He was looking for willing participants who would agree to and welcome His saving grace.

In our last lesson, we saw that unbelievers do not understand the message of the Gospel because, "…The god of this world hath blinded the minds of them which believe not, lest the light of the glorious gospel of Christ, who is the image of God, should shine unto them" (2 Corinthians 4:4). The word "blinded" — the Greek word *tuphlos* — indicates that Satan has gouged out the eyes of unbelievers so that they don't have eyes to see. But when the Gospel is shared through the mouth of an evangelist, the Holy Spirit miraculously creates spiritual eyes for unbelievers so they can see their dead spiritual condition and their need for Jesus.

After a person believes in and receives Jesus as their Lord and Savior, the Bible says they "…were sealed with that holy Spirit of promise" (Ephesians 1:13). The word "sealed" is the Greek word *sphragidzo*, which pictures *a seal placed on a package after the product had been thoroughly examined and inspected to make sure it was fully intact and complete*. The seal was proof the product was impeccable. Normally such seals bore the insignia of a wealthy or famous person, which meant that the package was to be treated with tender care. The seal affirmed who was the owner and guaranteed the package would make it to its final destination.

What does all this mean to you? It means that before you were given the Holy Spirit, God thoroughly checked you out and He made sure that your faith was intact and that everything inside you was impeccable. He then sealed you with the Holy Spirit.

Taking into account the original Greek meaning, here is the *Renner Interpretive Version (RIV)* of Ephesians 1:13:

> **When you were placed in Christ, God stamped you with a special seal and embossed it so deeply that it cannot be broken, erased, rubbed out, wiped out, deleted or removed; THAT unbreakable seal is the Holy Spirit. Once you were stamped with Him, it meant you had God's approval. He examined the contents of your heart and found nothing flawed or inferior.**
>
> **And because everything was in order, He stamped you with the Holy Spirit, which is His seal of approval. Anyone who has this stamp is headed for special treatment. THIS seal means you belong to God and no one is to interfere with you as a "package."**
>
> **This 'Holy Spirit stamp' means the postage is prepaid to get you all the way to your ultimate destination. That means you can be sure that once your journey with the Lord begins, you are going to make it all the way to where God wants you to go! As good as all of this already seems, it's only the beginning of what God has planned for us.**

The Holy Spirit Is the 'Earnest' of Your Inheritance

Paul continues to describe the Holy Spirit's actions in us in Ephesians 1:14, saying, "[He] is the earnest of our inheritance until the redemption of the purchased possession, unto the praise of his glory." The word "earnest" in this verse is the Greek word *arrabon*, and it describes *a payment given in advance to guarantee the whole amount will be paid afterward*. It is *earnest-money*, *an installment*, *a deposit*, or *a down-payment which guarantees full delivery of a promise*. Furthermore, it depicts *the security deposit given by the purchaser to assure confidence and peace to the seller that he will fulfill his promise.*

Taking into account the original Greek meaning, here is the *Renner Interpretive Version (RIV)* of Ephesians 1:14:

> **As good as all of this already seems, it's only the beginning of all that God has planned for us! The Holy Spirit is just the first-installment of the incredible things that God has planned as a part of our full inheritance. You might say the Holy Spirit is God's "down-money" to show that He is serious and intends to complete the deal, finalize all the papers, put the product in His name, and finally make us His very own possession, with no one else having the ability to exercise any claims or liens against us. When this process is finally wrapped up and the deal is completely sealed, we're going to all want to stand up and give God a round of applause for everything accomplished in our lives through His glory!**

So the Holy Spirit is God's seal of approval on our lives and the earnest of our inheritance. What is interesting is that Paul mentions these same two things in Second Corinthians 1:22, which says, "Who hath also sealed us, and given the earnest of the Spirit in our hearts." The word "sealed" here is the Greek word *sphragidzo*, and the word "earnest" is the Greek word *arrabon*.

Taking into account the original Greek meaning of these words, here is the *Renner Interpretive Version (RIV)* of Second Corinthians 1:22:

> **Who has stamped us with a special seal and embossed it so deeply that it cannot be broken, erased, rubbed out, wiped out, deleted or removed. Because we have that seal, it means we have God's approval. He has examined the contents of our hearts, found nothing flawed or inferior, and stamped us with the Holy Spirit as His seal of approval. Because we have this stamp, the postage has been prepaid to get us all the way to our ultimate destination. So we can be sure that once our journey with the Lord begins, we are going to make it all the way to where God wants us to go!**

Friend, God did it all. He is the One who initiated the process of our salvation, awakening us from spiritual death in our sins and giving us the ability to believe and receive Christ as our Lord and Savior. He gave us the power to become sons and daughters of God, and He made us His workmanship created in Christ Jesus to do good works. The day we were saved and received Christ into our life, God thoroughly inspected us and placed His seal of approval on us — the Holy Spirit. In that moment, our bodies became the temple of the Holy Spirit. And His seal guarantees everything inside of us is impeccable — nothing inferior, nothing flawed. We are God's and we're going to make it all the way to the end.

In our next lesson, we are going to examine the rich treasure that has been placed inside of you, which makes you a repository of God.

STUDY QUESTIONS

> **Study to shew thyself approved unto God, a workman that needeth not to be ashamed, rightly dividing the word of truth.**
> **— 2 Timothy 2:15**

1. Prior to this lesson, had you ever read the passage in John 20:19-22 where Jesus breathed on the disciples and told them to receive the Holy Spirit? If so, what did you understand this event to mean? How has this lesson expanded your understanding of this experience?
2. One of the benefits of having the seal of the Holy Spirit is that it ensures you make it safely all the way to your ultimate destination — Heaven. How do Second Timothy 1:12 and Jude 24 confirm this truth?

PRACTICAL APPLICATION

> **But be ye doers of the word, and not hearers only, deceiving your own selves.**
> **— James 1:22**

1. The Bible says that you were "sealed" with the Holy Spirit the moment you were saved. Carefully reread the meaning of the word "sealed" — the Greek word *sphragidzo*. What new encouraging insights is the Holy Spirit showing you about receiving God's seal of approval on your life?
2. Ephesians 1:14 tells us that the Holy Spirit is the "earnest of our inheritance." Take time to reflect on the meaning of the word "earnest"

— the Greek word *arrabon*. How does the meaning of this word instill hope in your heart and increase your trust in God's faithfulness?

LESSON 5

TOPIC

You Are a Repository of God's Greatest Treasure

SCRIPTURES

1. **1 Corinthians 6:19** — What? know ye not that your body is the temple of the Holy Ghost which is in you, which ye have of God, and ye are not your own?
2. **2 Corinthians 4:7-9** — But we have this treasure in earthen vessels, that the excellency of the power may be of God, and not of us. We are troubled on every side, yet not distressed; we are perplexed, but not in despair; persecuted, but not forsaken; cast down, but not destroyed.

GREEK WORDS

1. "body" — σῶμα (*soma*): the physical body
2. "temple" — ναός (*naos*): a temple or a highly decorated shrine; the image of vaulted ceilings, marble, granite, gold, silver, and highly decorated ornamentation; the most sacred, innermost part of a temple; the holy of holies
3. "in" — ἐν (*en*): literally, in or inside
4. "we have" — ἔχω (*echo*): to have, hold, or possess
5. "treasure" — θησαυρός (*thesauros*): a word describing a treasure, treasury, treasure chamber, or a place of safekeeping where riches and fortunes are kept; presents the idea of a specially built room designed to be the repository for massive riches and wealth
6. "earthen" — ὀστράκινος (*ostrakinos*): pottery made of inferior materials; fragile pottery; the word generally represented anything inferior, low-grade, mediocre, shoddy, second-rate, or substandard; the broken shards of pottery that were used for casting votes against citizens

who were banished from society; as a result, it meant to ostracize; it is where we get the word ostracize

7. "vessels" — σκεῦος (*skeuos*): a vessel, container, or utensil; could depict baggage, containers, equipment of various sorts, vases used in worship, kitchen items, or elegant articles of gold and silver put on public display; instruments

8. "excellency" — ὑπερβολή (*huperbole*): from ὑπερβάλλω (*huperballo*), something that is above and beyond what is normal; exceeding or surpassing; pictures an archer who aims his arrow at the target, but shoots way over the top; depicts something beyond the range of anything considered normal; something unparalleled

9. "power" — δύναμις (*dunamis*): power or ability; very often used to depict the assembled forces of an army whose combined strength enabled them to achieve unrivaled victories; these troops were so strong that they could not be resisted; generally depicts a power so mighty that it is impossible to resist or impossible to defeat

10. "troubled" — θλίβω (*thlibo*): from θλῖψις (*thlipsis*), affliction; tribulation; trouble; great pressure; crushing pressure; suffocating pressure; a horribly tight, life-threatening squeeze

11. "distressed" — στενοχωρέω (*stenochoreo*): to crush; to severely cramp; to hem in; to be severely pressed from two sides

12. "perplexed" — ἀπορέω (*aporeo*): to be at wits' end; pictures one so confused that he can't figure out where he is, what he's doing, or what is happening around him; one who is completely bewildered by surrounding events

13. "in despair" — ἐξαπορέομαι (*exaporeomai*): no way out; describes one who feels trapped, or caught, or up against the wall, or pinned down, and hence, utterly hopeless

14. "persecuted" — διώκω (*dioko*): to hunt, to chase, or to pursue; to persecute

15. "forsaken" — ἐγκαταλείπω (*engkataleipo*): discouraged, defeated, and depressed; emotions of one who feels left out, down, depressed, and far behind everyone else

16. "cast down" — καταβάλλω (*kataballo*): to throw down; to forcibly hurl down

17. "destroyed" — ἀπόλλυμι (*apollumi*): total loss; pictures full destruction; liquidation

SYNOPSIS

The construction of the Peter and Paul Cathedral in Saint Petersburg, Russia, began in 1712 and took about two decades to complete. This shrine was designed to be the final resting place for each member of the Romanov family who ruled the Russian Empire until the Bolshevik Revolution in 1917. It is a rich repository of precious stones and precious metals and is lavishly decorated with more than 22 pounds of gold.

Yet, as beautiful as this cathedral is, it pales in comparison to the priceless treasure God has placed inside of you. In Second Corinthians 4:7, Paul said, "But we have this treasure in earthen vessels, that the excellency of the power may be of God, and not of us." Friend, you are the repository of God's greatest treasure. You are the place He has deposited His Holy Spirit, and it is vital that you grasp just how valuable you are!

The emphasis of this lesson:

As the temple of the Holy Spirit, we have God's immense and inexhaustible treasure inside of us. The excellency of His power surges within us. Although we may be troubled and perplexed, we are not distressed or in despair. And while we are sometimes persecuted and cast down, we are not forsaken or destroyed.

A Summary of Our Anchor Verse

In the previous lessons, we have looked at Paul's declaration in First Corinthians 6:19, which says, "What? know ye not that your body is the temple of the Holy Ghost which is in you, which ye have of God, and ye are not your own?" This verse expresses Paul's amazement that the Corinthian believers did not yet understand or comprehend what God had made them to be.

The word "body" here is the Greek word *soma*, and it describes *the physical, human body*. The word "temple" is the Greek word *naos*, which describes *a temple or a highly decorated shrine*. It is the image of vaulted ceilings, marble, granite, gold, silver, and highly decorated ornamentation. It is the exact same word used in the Old Testament Septuagint to describe *the most sacred, innermost part of the temple in Jerusalem; the Holy of Holies*. By using the word *naos* — translated here as "temple" — God is saying that He fashioned our human bodies to become the holy of holies for His Spirit.

First Corinthians 6:19 says, "…Your body is the temple of the Holy Ghost which is in you…." The word "in" is the Greek word *en*, and it identifies that the location of this temple is inside of us. Hence, there is more to you than meets the eye. If your spiritual eyes were opened, you would be flabbergasted by all the lavish décor inside of you!

We Have God's Treasure in 'Earthen Vessels'

The apostle Paul builds on the idea of our bodies being temples of the Holy Spirit in Second Corinthians 4:7, saying, "But we have this treasure in earthen vessels, that the excellency of the power may be of God, and not of us."

Notice that Paul began this verse with the words "we have." In Greek, this is the plural form of the word *echo*, which means *to have, to hold*, or *to possess*. The word "treasure" is the Greek word *thesauros*, and it describes *a treasure, treasury, treasure chamber, or a place of safekeeping where riches and fortunes are kept*. It presents the idea of *a specially built room designed to be the repository for massive riches and wealth*.

A beautiful illustration of the word *thesauros* — treasure — would be the tombs of the pharaohs, which are located in the Valley of the Kings along the Nile River. Upon entering these immense chambers, one can see that the walls are covered with intricate hieroglyphs and paintings. Riches and precious jewels abound as far as the eye can see. One such tomb is the tomb of King Tut, which was discovered by archeologist Howard Carter in November 1922. When he first drilled a hole into that tomb and looked inside, he was blown away by all the marvelous things he saw.

The Bible says that *you* are just like one of these treasure chambers. You *have*, you *hold*, and you *possess* the treasure of God's Spirit in "earthen vessels." The word "vessels" is the Greek word *skeuos*, and it describes *a vessel, container*, or *utensil*. It can also depict *baggage, containers, equipment of various sorts, vases used in worship, kitchen items, or elegant articles of gold and silver put on public display*.

The word "earthen" is the Greek word *ostrakinos*, and it describes *fragile pottery made of inferior materials*. It was *inexpensive, flawed pottery that was covered with beautiful decorative paint*, and people loved it because it could be easily replaced if it broke. Thus, the word *ostrakinos* generally represented *anything inferior, low-grade, mediocre, shoddy, second-rate, or substandard.* What's interesting is that the broken shards of this *ostrakinos* pottery were used for casting votes against citizens who were banished from society. As a result, this process became known as *ostracizing* someone, which is from where we get the word *ostracize.*

It is not an accident that the Holy Spirit moved on the apostle Paul to use the words *ostrakinos* and *skeuos* — translated as "earthen vessels" — to describe our human bodies as containers of God's Spirit. The fact is, our bodies are just like *ostrakinos* pottery. Although we decorate them with beautiful clothing and cosmetics, they are nevertheless fragile, inferior, low-grade, mediocre, shoddy, second-rate, substandard, and flawed. Amazingly, God chose to place His "treasure" — the Greek word *thesauros* — inside of us. The inexhaustible treasure of His Spirit — which is wealth beyond imagination — has been deposited within us.

The 'Excellency of God's Power' Lives Within Us

Looking again at Second Corinthians 4:7, it says, "But we have this treasure in earthen vessels, that the excellency of the power may be of God, and not of us." The word "excellency" here is the Greek word *huperbole*, which is from the word *huperballo*. It describes *something that is above and beyond what is normal*; *something exceeding or surpassing*. It is the word used to picture an archer who aims his arrow at the target, but shoots way over the top of it. Hence, it depicts *something beyond the range of anything considered normal*; *something unparalleled*. Paul used this word to describe the riches and power that are inside of us. They are *exceeding, surpassing,* and *beyond our wildest imagination.*

This brings us to the word "power," which is the Greek word *dunamis*. It describes *power* or *ability* and was very often used to depict *the assembled forces of an army whose combined strength enabled them to achieve unrivaled victories.* These troops were so strong that they could not be resisted. Moreover, the word *dunamis* — translated here as "power" — generally depicts *a power so mighty that it is impossible to resist or impossible to defeat.*

Paul said that we need to understand what we have on the inside of us. God has fashioned us *to have, to hold,* and *to possess* in our "earthen vessels" — *ostrakinos* — the amazing exceeding and surpassing treasure and power of His Holy Spirit. We are treasure chambers that contain the unrivaled strength of Almighty God, and one of our primary tasks is to explore and unearth the riches of His Spirit that has been deposited within us so that we can truly enjoy the gift we have and share it with the world.

We Are Troubled and Perplexed But Not Distressed or in Despair

Paul went on to say, "We are troubled on every side, yet not distressed; we are perplexed, but not in despair" (2 Corinthians 4:8). The word "troubled" is the Greek word *thlibo*, which is a form of the Greek word *thlipsis*, and it describes *affliction*; *tribulation*; *trouble*; *great pressure*; *crushing pressure*; or a *suffocating pressure*. We could translate it as *a horribly tight, life-threatening squeeze*.

The Bible says that while we are troubled on every side, we are not "distressed." In Greek, this is the word *stenochoreo*, and it means *to crush*; *to severely cramp*; *to hem in*; or *to be severely pressed from two sides*. Furthermore, it says, "...We are perplexed, but not in despair" (2 Corinthians 4:8). The word "perplexed" in Greek is *aporeo*, which means *to be at wits' end*. It pictures *one so confused that he can't figure out where he is, what he's doing, or what is happening around him*.

Thankfully, even though we may be "perplexed" and *completely bewildered by surrounding events*, we are not "in despair." The phrase "in despair" is a translation of the Greek word *exaporeomai*, which means *no way out*. It describes *one who feels trapped, or caught, or up against the wall, or pinned down, and hence, utterly hopeless*. Even though we face situations in which we are perplexed — *aporeo* — and confused about what is happening around us, we are not "in despair" — we are *not* trapped, pinned down, or utterly hopeless.

We Are Persecuted and Cast Down But Not Forsaken or Destroyed

To all this Paul added that we are "persecuted, but not forsaken..." (2 Corinthians 4:9). The word "persecuted" in Greek is a translation of the hunting term *dioko*, which means *to hunt, to chase, or to pursue*. Although we are sometimes *hunted* and *pursued* like animals, we are not "forsaken." In Greek, the word "forsaken" is the word *engkataleipo*, and it describes *one who is discouraged, defeated, and depressed*. This means that while we may be persecuted, we don't *feel left out, down, depressed, and far behind everyone else*.

Furthermore, Paul said that we are "...cast down, but not destroyed" (2 Corinthians 4:9). The phrase "cast down" is the Greek word *kataballo*, which means *to throw down* or *to forcibly hurl down*. By using this word, Paul lets us know that there will be times in our lives when we are viciously attacked and hurled to the ground. Yet, he said we are not "destroyed." In Greek, "destroyed" is the word *apollumi*, and it describes *a total loss*. It pictures *full destruction* or *liquidation*. So, although we may be "cast down," we are never fully destroyed.

In the natural, the apostle Paul had been through so many difficult and trying situations, he should have been totally wiped out and utterly destroyed. But he wasn't because he learned how to draw upon the immense, inexhaustible treasure and surpassing power of God's greatness that was living within him. Even though he knew he was just an earthen vessel (*ostrakinos*), he also knew that he was the temple of the Holy Spirit!

In our next lesson, we will explore what it means to be a brand-new creature in Christ.

STUDY QUESTIONS

> **Study to shew thyself approved unto God, a workman that needeth not to be ashamed, rightly dividing the word of truth.**
> **— 2 Timothy 2:15**

1. The Bible says again and again that we are the temple of the Holy Spirit and that the *excellency of the power* of God dwells within us (*see* 2 Corinthians 4:7). How do John 1:16; Colossians 2:10; and Ephesians 3:20 reaffirm this truth? (Also consider Second Peter 1:3.)
2. God doesn't want you to just *know* about His power in your head. He wants you to *experience* His power in your everyday life. That is what the apostle Paul prayed for in Ephesians 3:14-19. Take a few moments to reflect on this prayer and make it a prayer of your own.

PRACTICAL APPLICATION

> **But be ye doers of the word, and not hearers only, deceiving your own selves.**
> **— James 1:22**

1. Second Corinthians 4:7 declares, "We have this treasure in earthen vessels...." Carefully reread the meaning of the word "earthen," which is the Greek word *ostrakinos*. What new insights about God's Spirit living in you have you learned from the meaning of this word?
2. God's Word also tells us that we are filled with the "excellency of His power" (*see* 2 Corinthians 4:7). Take time to review the meaning of these words in Greek. In what specific ways does this encourage you and strengthen your faith?
3. Do you really know and understand that your body is the temple of the Holy Spirit? Do you really have a revelation of who God has made you to be? Take a few moments to pray and ask God to open your spiritual eyes so that you have a fresh awareness of what it means to be the "temple of the Holy Spirit."

LESSON 6

TOPIC
You Are a Brand-New Creature

SCRIPTURES
1. **1 Corinthians 6:19** — What? know ye not that your body is the temple of the Holy Ghost which is in you, which ye have of God, and ye are not your own?
2. **2 Corinthians 5:17-19** — Therefore if any man be in Christ, he is a new creature: old things are passed away; behold, all things are become new. And all things are of God, who hath reconciled us to himself by Jesus Christ, and hath given to us the ministry of reconciliation; to wit, that God was in Christ, reconciling the world unto himself, not imputing their trespasses unto them; and hath committed unto us the word of reconciliation.

GREEK WORDS
1. "What" — ἤ (*e*): an exclamation
2. "know ye not" — οὐκ οἴδατε (*ouk oidate*): from οὐκ (*ouk*) and οἶδα (*oida*); the word οὐκ (*ouk*) is an emphatic no, and οἶδα (*oida*), to see,

perceive, understand, or comprehend; the word οἶδα (*oida*) depicts knowledge gained by personal experience or personal observation; in this verse, have you not emphatically comprehended

3. "that" — ὅτι (*hoti*): points to an important point
4. "body" — σῶμα (*soma*): the physical body
5. "temple" — ναός (*naos*): a temple or a highly decorated shrine; the image of vaulted ceilings, marble, granite, gold, silver, and highly decorated ornamentation; the most sacred, innermost part of a temple; the holy of holies
6. "in" — ἐν (*en*): literally, in or inside
7. "ye have" — ἔχω (*echo*): to have, hold, or possess
8. "of" — ἀπό (*apo*): from, as directly from God
9. "new" — καινός (*kainos*): something that is brand new or recently made; not fixed or repaired, but brand new; carries the idea of something that is superior
10. "creature" — κτίσις (*ktisis*): creation of something from nothing; not renewed or refashioned with old material, but brand-spanking new and never existing before; not enhanced, improved, repaired, or restored; something newly created and original
11. "old things" — ἀρχαῖος (*archaios*): ancient; archaic; primitive; obsolete; outdated; old; what used to be
12. "passed away" — παρέρχομαι (*parerchomai*): to pass into the past; rendered void; disregarded; no longer applicable
13. "behold" — ἰδού (*idou*): bewilderment, shock, amazement, and wonder
14. "become" — γίνομαι (*ginomai*): to suddenly become; to transition from one thing to another
15. "reconciled" — καταλλάσσω (*katallasso*): a total transformation from top to bottom
16. "given" — δίδωμι (*didomi*): to give into one's care; to entrust; to commit
17. "ministry" — διακονίαν (*diakonian*): from διάκονος (*diakonos*), a high-level servant; sophisticated and highly trained servants who serve the needs of others; a servant whose primary responsibility is to serve food and wait on tables; pictures a waiter or waitress who painstakingly attends to the needs, wishes, and desires of his or her client; servants who professionally pleased clients; a type of serving that was honorable, pleasurable, and done in a fashion that made people being served feel as if they were nobility

18. "reconciliation" — καταλλαγή (*katallage*): reconciliation; transformation
19. "committed" — θέμενος (*themenos*): from τίθημι (*tithemi*), to established, fix, place, position, or put into place
20. "the word" — τὸν λόγον (*ton logon*): the word; the message

SYNOPSIS

Another magnificent cathedral in Saint Petersburg, Russia, is the Resurrection of Christ Church, which is also known as the Church on Spilled Blood. The history behind this cathedral dates back to 1881 when Alexander II was traveling in his carriage to the Winter Palace, and while he was in route, a terrorist threw a bomb under his carriage. The explosion badly damaged the wagon, killing three people and wounding several others.

Immediately, Alexander emerged from the carriage to see if he could help those who had survived. When the terrorist saw him step out unharmed, he threw another bomb, which exploded just below his feet and blew off his legs. Rescuers quickly picked him up and carried him into the Winter Palace. But within a few hours, Alexander II was pronounced dead.

His son, Alexander III, gave an order for a church to be built on the place where his father's blood had been spilled. Hence, the local people came to call it the Church on Spilled Blood. The formal name of the cathedral is the Resurrection of Christ Church, and it is simply remarkable.

In 1907, it was officially consecrated, and the ceremony was attended by Emperor Nicholas II, his wife Alexandra, and their children. The floor of this incredible cathedral is composed of 16 different types of marble that was created in Florence, Italy. Equally impressive are the more than 300 mosaics of biblical characters that were created in a local workshop in Saint Petersburg.

When people enter the Resurrection of Christ Church, they are usually overwhelmed by its beauty because they have never seen so many mosaics. The fact is, there are more than 71,000 square feet of glistening mosaics in this church that tell the story of the life and ministry of Jesus.

As breathtaking as this cathedral is, it is no match for the spiritual interiors you possess. The moment you surrendered your life to Christ and invited Him into your life, God transformed you into an amazing temple for His Spirit to live in. Now you carry the presence of God with you everywhere you go. In Christ, you are a brand-new creature!

The emphasis of this lesson:

The moment you surrender your life to Christ, you become a new creature. God does not rehabilitate, refurbish, or repair the old you. He disregards your old nature and renders it void, and He makes you into something brand-spanking new.

A Review of Our Anchor Verse

Writing to the believers in Corinth and Christians everywhere, the apostle Paul said, "What? Know ye not that your body is the temple of the Holy Ghost which is in you, which ye have of God, and ye are not your own?" (1 Corinthians 6:19)

As we have seen, this verse begins with the word "what," which in Greek is an exclamation. It's the equivalent of Paul saying, "What! What is this?" Then he said, "Know ye not," which in Greek is *ouk oidate*. It is taken from the word *ouk*, which is *an emphatic no*, and the word *oida*, which means *to see, perceive, understand, or comprehend*. It depicts *knowledge gained by personal experience or personal observation*. In this verse, the phrase "know ye not" means, "Have you not emphatically comprehended?"

Basically, Paul asked, "Have you not yet gotten it? Do you not understand that your body is the temple of the Holy Ghost?" The Greek word for "body" here is *soma*, and it describes *the physical body*. The moment we were saved, God miraculously transformed our bodies into a temple for His Spirit to dwell. We have seen that the word "temple" is the Greek word *naos* — a term any Greek reader would understand, including the Corinthian Christians who were Greeks. The word *naos* — translated here as "temple" — describes *a highly decorated shrine*.

The city of Corinth had many pagan temples, and if you had gone into any one of them, you would have seen their lavish decor. They would have had vaulted ceilings, marble, granite, gold, silver, and highly decorated ornamentation. Paul chose the word *naos* to describe you as God's temple. It is actually the same word used in the Old Testament Septuagint to describe *the innermost part of the temple in Jerusalem* or *the Holy of Holies*.

Paul said, "What? Do you not get it? You have become the *naos* — the highly-decorated shrine — of the Holy Spirit." The truth is, if your eyes were opened and you could observe your spiritual interiors, you would see that inwardly you have been lavishly decorated with the power of God, the gifts of the Holy Spirit, the matchless blood of Jesus, and the very character of God Himself.

The Bible says that all these things are "in" us. In Greek, the word "in" is the word *en*, and it pinpoints the location of God's greatest treasure; it is *inside* us. Paul went on to say, "…which ye have of God." The word "of" in Greek is the word *apo*, and it means *directly coming from God*. Therefore, what took place in us the day we were saved is not the result of our personal rehabilitation or us reforming ourselves. The transformation we experienced came directly from — *apo* — God. It is a result of God's divine work of grace in our lives.

We know from Ephesians 2:1 that when God found us, we "…were dead in trespasses and sins" and powerless to do anything on our own to change it. "But God, who is rich in mercy, for his great love wherewith he loved us, even when we were dead in sins, hath quickened us together with Christ…" (Ephesians 2:4,5). God was the initiator of our salvation; it had nothing to do with us. That is why Paul went on to say, "For by grace are ye saved through faith; and that not of yourselves: it is the gift of God: not of works, lest any man should boast" (Ephesians 2:8,9).

Friend, God did it all, and all we had to do was say yes to Jesus when He came knocking on our heart's door. Once we did, the Bible says in that moment we became God's "workmanship," which in the Greek literally means we became His *masterpiece* (*see* Ephesians 2:10). The Holy Spirit moved inside of us, and we became the temple of the Holy Spirit.

You Are a 'New Creature' in Christ

The apostle Paul describes the powerful transformation that took place in our lives in Second Corinthians 5:17, which says, "Therefore if any man be in Christ, he is a new creature: old things are passed away; behold, all things are become new."

The word "new" here is the Greek word *kainos*, and it describes *something that is brand new or recently made*. It is not something that has been fixed, enhanced, or repaired, but *brand new*. This word carries the idea of *something that is superior*. This means when Jesus Christ came into your life, you were made brand-spanking new! The new you is superior to the old you! In fact, you are so new that this verse calls you a new "creature."

The word "creature" in this verse is the Greek word *ktisis*, and it describes *the creation of something from nothing*. It is not something renewed or refashioned with old material, but *brand-spanking new and never existing before*. It is not enhanced, improved, repaired, or restored; it is *something newly created and original*. Actually, the word *ktisis* — translated here as "creature" — is the same word used to describe the creation of the world. When God created the universe, He didn't use any existing materials or old elements to make it. Everything in creation was newly made.

Now this word *ktisis* describes what happened to you the day you got saved. Everything about you is new! You're not an amended, corrected, improved version of what you used to be. There was nothing in your old nature worth salvaging. When the power of God came upon you, you became an absolutely brand-new creation! You are completely detached from the person you once were before Christ.

Old Things Are Passed Away

After declaring that you are a "new creature" in Christ, Paul said, "…old things are passed away…" (2 Corinthians 5:17). The Greek word for "old things" is *archaios*, which is from where we get the word *archaic*. It describes *something ancient, archaic, primitive, obsolete, outdated, old,* or *what used to be*. The moment you were saved, the old, primitive, outdated you "passed away."

The phrase "passed away" in Greek is *parerchomai*, and it means *to pass into the past, to be rendered void*. It carries the idea of being *disregarded* or *no longer applicable*. The old "you" is not who you are today; it has been rendered void and is permanently gone. Paul said, when you surrendered your life to Christ, "…behold, all things are become new" (2 Corinthians 5:17).

The word "behold" is the Greek word *idou*, which is an expression of *bewilderment, shock, amazement, and wonder*. By using this word, Paul is actually interjecting his feelings into the text. It is almost as if he is saying, "Wow! This is absolutely amazing! I'm almost at a loss of words because I'm so excited."

Then he said, "…All things become new." The word "become" is the Greek word *ginomai*, which means *to suddenly become*. It describes *a transition from one thing to another*. This means what is being described here is not a process of rehabilitation but an *instantaneous* change. All things *suddenly* become new.

The word "new" is once again the Greek word *kainos*, meaning *something that is brand new or recently made*. It is not something that is fixed or repaired, but *brand new*. It carries the idea of *something that is superior* and nothing in comparison to what it used to be. The old you is outdated, archaic, and no longer applicable. By God's limitless mercy and grace, He has remade you into something that has never existed before. You are His masterpiece created in Christ Jesus to do good works (*see* Ephesians 2:10).

We Were 'Reconciled' to God and Given the 'Ministry of Reconciliation'

In Second Corinthians 5:18, Paul went on to say, "And all things are of God, who hath reconciled us to himself by Jesus Christ, and hath given to us the ministry of reconciliation. The word "reconciled" is the Greek word *katallasso*, and it describes *a total transformation from top to bottom*. This indicates that when you were saved, Christ totally transformed you from the inside out, from top to bottom.

Along with our transformation, Paul said we were "given" the ministry of reconciliation. This word "given" in Greek is *didomi*, which means *to give into one's care*; *to entrust*; or *to commit*. It says we were entrusted with the "ministry of reconciliation." The word "reconciliation" is the Greek word *katallage*, and it, too, refers to *transformation*, not rehabilitation. Basically, God has given to us the responsibility to share about His transforming power with others. It is our ongoing "ministry."

In Greek, the word "ministry" is the word *diakonian*, which was taken from the word *diakonos*, and it depicts *a high-level servant who is sophisticated and highly trained to serve the needs of others*. This word *diakonos* denotes *a servant whose primary responsibility is to serve food and wait on tables*. It pictures *a waiter or waitress who painstakingly attends to the needs, wishes, and desires of his or her client*. It carries the idea of *servants who professionally pleased clients* or *a type of serving that was honorable, pleasurable, and done in a fashion that made people being served as if they were nobility*.

Once God reconciled you to Himself — totally transforming you from top to bottom — He gave you the ministry of reconciliation. That is, He entrusted you with the responsibility to become a sophisticated, highly-trained servant who is committed to the ministry of transformation in the lives of others.

God Offers Transformation — Not Rehabilitation

The apostle Paul continued by saying, "To wit, that God was in Christ, reconciling the world unto himself, not imputing their trespasses unto them; and hath committed unto us the word of reconciliation" (2 Corinthians 5:19). Here again we see Paul saying something very similar to what he said in verse 18.

After we are reconciled to God, He "…committed unto us the word of reconciliation" (2 Corinthians 5:19). The word "committed" is the Greek word *themenos*, which is from the word *tithemi*, meaning *to establish, fix, place, position, or put into place*. Thus, God has established and positioned us in a place where we are to offer the "word of reconciliation."

The phrase "the word" in Greek is *ton logon*, and it means *the word* or *the message*. The Greek word for "reconciliation" is once again *katallage*, which describes *reconciliation* or *total transformation*. This lets us know that when we share the Gospel with the unsaved, we need to help them understand that what God is offering through Jesus is *not* rehabilitation, personal enhancement, or improving and repairing who they are. What God is offering by His grace and through the blood of Jesus is a brand-new beginning — where the old man is done away with and He completely transforms us from top to bottom!

Remember, "…Your body is the temple of the Holy Ghost which is in you, which ye have of God…" (1 Corinthians 6:19). This powerful transformation into a highly decorated shrine (*naos*) for the Holy Spirit is totally the result of God's will and God's work. In our next lesson, we will discover how all believers together make up the corporate temple of the Holy Spirit.

STUDY QUESTIONS

> **Study to shew thyself approved unto God, a workman that needeth not to be ashamed, rightly dividing the word of truth.**
> **— 2 Timothy 2:15**

1. From start to finish, our salvation is totally a result of God's will and His work in our lives. Out of great gratitude for what He did, what does the Bible say our response should be?
   - 2 Corinthians 5:15 and Galatians 2:20
   - Romans 8:12; 12:1; and 13:14

- Colossians 3:1-3 and Ephesians 4:22-24

2. The Bible says God has given us the "ministry of reconciliation," which means we are to share with others about the transforming power of God. According to First Peter 3:15, how are you to prepare for this ongoing assignment? (Also consider Mark 5:18,19.)

PRACTICAL APPLICATION

> **But be ye doers of the word, not hearers only, deceiving your own selves.**
> —James 1:22

1. In your own words, what does it mean to be a "new creature" in Christ? What were some of the obvious "new" things you noticed in your life right after you got saved? What aspects of your old life immediately "passed away" and left you drastically different?
2. If you had sixty seconds to talk to an unsaved person that you know you would never see again, what would you tell them about God's love and mercy and how He transformed your life by the power of His Spirit?

LESSON 7

TOPIC

You Are the Corporate Temple of the Holy Spirit

SCRIPTURES

1. **1 Corinthians 6:19,20** — What? know ye not that your body is the temple of the Holy Ghost which is in you, which ye have of God, and ye are not your own? For ye are bought with a price: therefore glorify God in your body, and in your spirit, which are God's.
2. **1 Corinthians 3:16,17** — Know ye not that ye are the temple of God, and that the Spirit of God dwelleth in you? If any man defile the temple of God, him shall God destroy; for the temple of God is holy, which temple ye are.

GREEK WORDS

1. "What" — ἤ (*e*): an exclamation
2. "know ye not" — οὐκ οἴδατε (*ouk oidate*): from οὐκ (*ouk*) and οἶδα (*oida*); the word οὐκ (*ouk*) is an emphatic no, and οἶδα (*oida*), to see, perceive, understand, or comprehend; the word οἶδα (*oida*) depicts knowledge gained by personal experience or personal observation; in this verse, have you not emphatically comprehended
3. "that" — ὅτι (*hoti*): points to an important point
4. "body" — σῶμα (*soma*): the physical body
5. "temple" — ναός (*naos*): a temple or a highly decorated shrine; the image of vaulted ceilings, marble, granite, gold, silver, and highly decorated ornamentation; the most sacred, innermost part of a temple; the holy of holies
6. "in" — ἐν (*en*): literally, in or inside
7. "ye have" — ἔχω (*echo*): to have, hold, or possess
8. "of" — ἀπό (*apo*): from, as directly from God
9. "not your own" — οὐκ ἐστὲ ἑαυτῶν (*ouk este heauton*): "emphatically not your own"
10. "bought" — ἀγοράζω (*agoradzo*): to purchase in the marketplace; often used to denote the purchase of a slave out of the slave market; to transfer ownership from a seller to a buyer; to redeem
11. "price" — τιμή (*time*): price; value; worth; price that which is costly and extremely valuable; literally, at a great price
12. "therefore" — δή (*de*): consequently; subsequently; as a result
13. "glorify" — δοξάζω (*doxadzo*): from δοκέω (*dokeo*), to think or to estimate; honor; value; to show weight and worth
14. "dwelleth" — οἰκέω (*oikeo*): dwell in a house; take up residency; settle into a home; to be at home; to be a permanent indweller
15. "any" — τις (*tis*): any one; any person
16. "defile" — φθείρω (*phtheiro*): waste; corrupt; deteriorate; figuratively to cause a moral deterioration; a decomposition or break-down; to move from a higher level to a lower level
17. "destroy" — φθείρω (*phtheiro*): waste; corrupt; deteriorate; figuratively to cause a moral deterioration; a decomposition or break-down; to move from a higher level to a lower level
18. "holy" — ἅγιος (*hagios*): holy, consecrated, different, separate, special

SYNOPSIS

The Resurrection of Christ Church in Saint Petersburg, Russia, was officially opened and consecrated in 1907. But after the communist regime came to power, the church was closed in the 1930s. Initially, this fabulous building began to be used as a warehouse for potatoes. Then the communist regime decided they would blow up the building and completely demolish it, but that plan was stopped by the onset of the events of World War II.

During the war, this cathedral — which was also known as the Church on Spilled Blood — was used as a morgue for the dead. After the war, it was turned into a huge warehouse for storing props for a local theatrical company amongst other things. Eventually, it fell into ruin, but it was renovated and reopened in 1997 as an official museum of Russian history.

The walls of the Resurrection of Christ Church are covered with more than 71,000 square feet of beautiful mosaics, which were created in a mosaic workshop in the city of Saint Petersburg. What's fascinating about these mosaics is that they each tell a story in the life of Jesus. One shows Jesus casting out a demon, and another shows Him healing the woman with the issue of blood. There is also a mosaic of Jesus multiplying the loaves and the fishes and one of His miracle of walking on the water. There is even a depiction of the Day of Pentecost.

To think that this magnificent church had been abandoned for so many years and was almost destroyed is simply mind boggling. Nevertheless, today it has been splendidly restored to its original magnificence, and it serves as one of the most popular tourist stops in the city of Saint Petersburg, Russia.

Again, as beautiful as this cathedral is, it doesn't hold a candle to the beauty of the temple God has made you to be. The Bible says that as an individual believer, you are the temple of the Holy Spirit (*see* 1 Corinthians 6:19). It also says that all believers collectively make up the corporate temple of the Holy Spirit (*see* 1 Corinthians 3:16). It is God's people that form God's Church. *We* are His holy habitation — not a building — and He literally lives in us and among us.

The emphasis of this lesson:

In addition to each individual believer being the temple of the Holy Spirit, the Church as a whole is also God's temple. God calls His temple

holy — it is consecrated, separated, and special in His sight. The way we treat His temple is the way He will treat us.

A Review of Our Anchor Verse

In First Corinthians 6:19, the apostle Paul wrote the believers and said, "What? Know ye not that your body is the temple of the Holy Ghost which is in you, which ye have of God, and ye are not your own?" The reason he wrote this to the believers in Corinth is because they were doing things they shouldn't have been doing, such as going to sinful places and connecting with prostitutes.

When you read this verse in the Greek, the word "what" is actually an exclamation. It is as if Paul said, "What! What is this? How is this humanly possible?" He then said, "Know ye not," which in Greek is *ouk oidate* and is derived from the word *ouk*, which is *an emphatic no*, and the word *oida*, which means *to see, perceive, understand, or comprehend*. Altogether, the phrase "know ye not" is the equivalent of saying, "Do you not yet know? Have you not really comprehended? Do you not yet understand?"

What was Paul so astonished that they didn't know? He said, "That your body is the temple of the Holy Ghost?" The Greek word for "body" here is *soma*, and it describes *the physical body*. The moment you were saved, God miraculously transformed your body into a temple for His Spirit to dwell in. We have seen that the word "temple" is the Greek word *naos*, and it describes *a highly decorated shrine*.

The city of Corinth was filled with many pagan temples, and the Corinthian Christians were very familiar with their lavish interiors. They had vaulted ceilings, marble, granite, gold, silver, and highly decorated ornamentation. Paul chose the word *naos* to describe each of us as God's temple. It is the exact same word used in the Old Testament Septuagint to describe *the innermost part of the temple in Jerusalem — the Holy of Holies*.

Paul said, "What? Do you not get it? Don't you realize you have become the *naos* — the *highly-decorated shrine* — of the Holy Spirit. You shouldn't be going where you're going and doing the things you're doing with your bodies. You are the living, breathing sanctuary of God's Spirit!" The truth is, if your eyes were opened and you could see what you look like in the spirit, you would discover that inwardly you have been extravagantly adorned with all of God's power and character. He moved inside of you the day you gave your life to Him, and *you* became His Holy of Holies.

The Bible says that the Spirit of God is "in" us. The word "in" is the Greek word *en*, and it identifies that the location of God's greatest treasure is *inside* us. Paul went on to say, "…Which ye have of God…" (1 Corinthians 6:19). The phrase "ye have" is a form of the Greek word *echo*, which means *to have, to hold, or to possess*. It pictures us as *containers* of God. Moreover, the word "of" is the Greek word *apo*, and it means *directly coming from God*. Hence, what happened the day we were saved is not the result of any effort on our part. The transformation we experienced came directly from (*apo*) God.

Paul wrapped up First Corinthians 6:19 by saying, "…Ye are not your own," which means we should live with a sense of responsibility and indebtedness to God for all that He has brought about in our lives. Everything is the result of His divine work of grace in our lives.

You Are 'Bought With a Price'

When we come to First Corinthians 6:20, Paul continued his discussion with the Corinthian believers, saying, "For ye are bought with a price: therefore glorify God in your body, and in your spirit, which are God's." Notice the word "bought." It is the Greek word *agoradzo*, which is from where we get the word *agora*, the word for a *marketplace*. Thus, the word *agoradzo* means *to purchase in the marketplace*.

What is interesting about this word is that it was often used to denote *the purchase of a slave out of the slave market*. In the First Century, the slave market was a disgusting and deplorable place. Human beings were placed on auction blocks and sold to the highest bidder. These slaves were often abused and traded back and forth between masters — keeping them trapped in slavery for the rest of their lives.

Basically, the Bible teaches us that when Jesus came into the world, He entered into Satan's slave market where the entire human race was bound in slavery to sin. As our slave master, Satan abused us and traded us from one form of bondage to another. But when Jesus came, He paid the ultimate price to buy us back and set us free from our slavery to Satan and to sin. That is the picture of the word *agoradzo* — translated here as "bought." It means *to redeem*; *to transfer ownership from a seller to a buyer*.

Paul told the Corinthian believers — *and us* — that we have been bought with a "price." The word "price" is the Greek word *time*, and it means *price; value;* or *worth*. It denotes *that which is costly and extremely valuable*. The original Greek here would be better translated, "You were redeemed at a great price." The price that was paid to redeem you is the highest price ever paid for a slave. Jesus shed His blood and gave His life to buy you back and make you His own.

Glorify God in Your Spirit and Body

What should be our response to such an incredible sacrifice? Paul said, "...Therefore glorify God in your body, and in your spirit, which are God's" (1 Corinthians 6:20). The word "therefore" is the Greek word *de*, which means *consequently; subsequently;* or *as a result*. Basically, Paul said, "As a result of and in response to what Jesus did, glorify God."

The word "glorify" is the Greek word *doxadzo*. It is from the word *dokeo*, which means *to think* or *to estimate*. The use of this word tells us that in order to glorify God, we really need to *put our minds to it*. We can't be lackadaisical about it or just hope it happens. The word *dokeo* — translated here as "glorify" — can also mean *honor, value;* or *to show weight and worth*.

Now, when many believers hear, "...Therefore glorify God in your body, and in your spirit, which are God's" (1 Corinthians 6:20), they think, *Well, I'm already glorifying God in my spirit because that is where He lives.* Although this is true, this verse also says you are to glorify Him in your "body." Here again, is the Greek word *soma*, which describes *the physical human body*. When Jesus died, He not only purchased your spirit, He also purchased your body. Therefore, it is no longer yours but His, and He wants you to determine how you can best glorify Him with it. Remember, your body is *His* temple.

The Church Is Corporately the Temple of God

In First Corinthians 3:16, Paul addressed the entire church in Corinth and said, "Know ye not that ye are the temple of God, and that the Spirit of God dwelleth in you?" This lets us know that in addition to each believer being the temple of the Holy Spirit, the Church is also *corporately* a sanctuary for the Spirit of God.

What is interesting is that Paul uses the exact same words here in First Corinthians 3:16 that he used in First Corinthians 6:19. The phrase "know ye not" is once again the Greek words *ouk oidate*, which are from the words *ouk* and *oida*. The word *ouk* is *an emphatic no*, and the word *oida* means *to see, perceive, understand, or comprehend*. Taken together, the phrase "know ye not" is the equivalent of Paul saying, "Don't you get it? Have you not yet comprehended it? Do you not realize that as a church, you are corporately the temple of God?"

Once more we see the word "temple," which is the Greek word *naos*, and it describes *a temple or a highly decorated shrine*. It is the image of vaulted ceilings, marble, granite, gold, silver, and highly decorated ornamentation, and it is the same word used to describe *the most sacred, innermost part of a temple; the Holy of Holies*. Paul said that as a Church body, we form a huge place for God's Spirit to dwell.

This brings us to the word "dwelleth," which is the Greek word *oikeo*, and it means *to dwell in a house; to settle into a home;* or *to be at home*. It is the picture of *a person who takes up permanent residency, to be a permanent indweller*. This tells us that God has permanently moved into the Church, and we have become a massive, magnificent dwelling place for Him. He has settled down and made Himself at home in us corporately.

We Must Be Careful Not To 'Defile' God's Temple

The apostle Paul went on to say, "If any man defile the temple of God, him shall God destroy; for the temple of God is holy, which temple ye are" (1 Corinthians 3:17). This is quite a sobering warning. First, notice he said, "If any man." The word "any" is the Greek word *tis*, which means *any one; any person*. This Greek term is gender neutral and includes any male or any female.

Next, we see the word "defile," which is the Greek word *phtheiro*, and it means *to waste, corrupt,* or *deteriorate*. Figuratively, it means *to cause a moral deterioration*; it is *a decomposition or break down that causes something to move from a higher level to a lower level*. Thus, Paul is saying, "If any man or woman in the Church is a contributor to defiling the Church — causing it to deteriorate, become corrupt, or break down and move from a higher level to a lower level — him shall God destroy."

Interestingly, in this verse the word "destroy" and the word "defile" are the same Greek word — the word *phtheiro*. So when the Bible says, "Him shall God destroy," it literally means, "Him will God *waste, corrupt,* and *deteriorate.*" Any person — man or woman — that corrupts or causes the Church to break down and move from a higher level to a lower level, God Himself will cause to decompose and break down. In other words, God will do to him what he did to the Church. Remember, the Church is corporately the temple — *naos* — of the Holy Spirit of God, and He is highly protective of it.

A great example of what happens when a person defiles the Church is found in the book of First Samuel. As the book opens, we see Eli serving as the judge and high priest in Israel, and his sons, Hophni and Phinehas, were serving under him. But Hophni and Phinehas really did not know the Lord and they brought Him great dishonor. They were abusing the people who came to worship God by stealing God's offerings. To make matters worse, they were having sexual relations with the women who came to the door of the tabernacle.

The Bible says, "Wherefore the sin of the young men was very great before the Lord: for men abhorred the offering of the Lord" (1 Samuel 2:17). Basically, because of Hophni and Phinehas' actions, the people grew to hate coming to the tabernacle to worship God, and many of them simply stopped coming to church altogether. They were tired of being abused. These young men were wasting and corrupting the house of God and negatively affecting God's people.

A careful reading of the story reveals that God patiently tolerated the destructive behavior of Hophni and Phinehas for a long time. Even though they were in sin and doing wrong, He did not quickly bring judgment. The truth is, God is never in a rush to judge and dole out punishment. But when people's behavior becomes so foul that it detrimentally affects His Church, He steps in and brings judgment. The way Hophni and Phinehas dealt with God's house is the way God dealt with them — and their father Eli. For in one day, all three of them died (*see* 1 Samuel 4:11-18). This historical account is a strong warning that we must be careful how we treat God's temple and the people who corporately *are* the temple. "If any man defile the temple of God, him shall God destroy…" (1 Corinthians 3:17).

This verse goes on to say, "…For the temple of God is holy, which temple ye are" (1 Corinthians 3:17). The word "holy" here is the Greek word *hagios,* and it describes *something that is holy, consecrated, different, separate,* or *special*. This tells us that the house of God is different and special. It is consecrated and separated to be holy unto God.

Paul concludes First Corinthians 3:17 by saying, "...which temple ye are." He is not talking to each individual believer; he is talking to the entire church. Corporately, we are the temple of the Holy Spirit, and God has taken up permanent residency within us as His habitation.

STUDY QUESTIONS

> Study to shew thyself approved unto God, a workman that needeth not to be ashamed, rightly dividing the word of truth.
> — 2 Timothy 2:15

1. What happened the day we were saved is not the result of any effort on our part. Our salvation is the result of God's immeasurable love and grace. What does the Bible say in John 6:63; Romans 7:18; Isaiah 64:6 and 7 about our old nature — our flesh — and our abilities apart from God?
2. Why is it vital that we be reminded of this fact on a regular basis? Carefully consider Jesus' words in John 15:5; Paul's words in Philippians 3:3; and God's words in Zechariah 4:6 as you answer.
3. Take some time to reflect on the story of Eli and his sons, Hophni and Phinehas, in First Samuel 2:12-17,22-36 and First Samuel 4:11-18. As a parent or grandparent, what lessons can you learn from the life of Eli and apply in your own life? What can you learn from Hophni and Phinehas' example?

PRACTICAL APPLICATION

> But be ye doers of the word, and not hearers only, deceiving your own selves.
> —James 1:22

1. First Corinthians 6:20 says, "...Therefore glorify God in your body, and in your spirit, which are God's." In your own words, what would you say this looks like on a day-to-day basis? How are you personally glorifying God in your *body*? How about in your *spirit*?
2. Pause for a moment and pray: *"Lord, is there anything I'm currently doing in my spirit or in my body that is dishonoring You? If so, what is it?*

What can I do differently to truly bring You glory?" Listen carefully for the voice of the Holy Spirit and ask Him for the grace to do what He says.
3. Through the apostle Paul, God made it clear that we are individually His temple and collectively His temple. What is the significance between these two perspectives? Why do you think it is important for us to understand the difference?

LESSON 8

TOPIC
You Are Filled With the Riches of Christ

SCRIPTURES

1. **1 Corinthians 6:19,20** — What? know ye not that your body is the temple of the Holy Ghost which is in you, which ye have of God, and ye are not your own? For ye are bought with a price: therefore glorify God in your body, and in your spirit, which are God's.

2. **1 Corinthians 1:4-8** — I thank my God always on your behalf, for the grace of God which is given you by Jesus Christ; that in every thing ye are enriched by him, in all utterance, and in all knowledge; even as the testimony of Christ was confirmed in you: so that ye come behind in no gift; waiting for the coming of our Lord Jesus Christ: who shall also confirm you unto the end, that ye may be blameless in the day of our Lord Jesus Christ.

GREEK WORDS

1. "What" — ἤ (*e*): an exclamation
2. "know ye not" — οὐκ οἴδατε (*ouk oidate*): from οὐκ (*ouk*) and οἶδα (*oida*); the word οὐκ (*ouk*) is an emphatic no, and οἶδα (*oida*), to see, perceive, understand, or comprehend; the word οἶδα (*oida*) depicts knowledge gained by personal experience or personal observation; in this verse, have you not emphatically comprehended
3. "that" — ὅτι (*hoti*): points to an important point

4. "body" — σῶμα (*soma*): the physical body
5. "temple" — ναός (*naos*): a temple or a highly decorated shrine; the image of vaulted ceilings, marble, granite, gold, silver, and highly decorated ornamentation; the most sacred, innermost part of a temple; the holy of holies
6. "in" — ἐν (*en*): literally, in or inside
7. "ye have" — ἔχω (*echo*): to have, hold, or possess
8. "of" — ἀπό (*apo*): from, as directly from God
9. "not your own" — οὐκ ἐστὲ ἑαυτῶν (*ouk este heauton*): emphatically, "not your own"
10. "grace" — χάρις (*charis*): grace; historically, a favorable touch of the gods; in context, God's grace that supernaturally equips the recipient
11. "in every thing" — ἐν παντὶ (*en panti*): in every way; in every thing; an all-encompassing phrase
12. "enriched" — πλουτίζω (*ploutidzo*): wealth so great it cannot be tabulated; abundant wealth; vast wealth; extreme riches; incredible abundance; magnificent opulence; extravagant lavishness; used by Plato to say no one was richer than legendary King Midas
13. "utterance" — λόγος (*logos*): in all speech, referring to vocal gifts of the Holy Spirit; includes specifically word of knowledge, word of wisdom, prophecy, tongues, interpretation of tongues
14. "knowledge" — γνῶσις (*gnosis*): knowledge, refereeing to knowledge gifts of the Holy Spirit; includes word of wisdom, word of knowledge, prophecy, discerning of spirits
15. "testimony" — μαρτύριον (*marturion*): testimony; one who gives testimony in a court of law
16. "confirmed" — βεβαιόω (*bebaioo*): to authenticate; to verify; to establish or make concrete
17. "come behind" — ὑστερέω (*hustereo*): having a lack of sufficiency; a deficiency; a shortage; a shortfall
18. "coming" — ἀποκάλυψις (*apokalupsis*): refers to something that has been veiled or hidden, but then becomes clear and visible to the mind or eye; an unveiling; a sudden revealing; to uncover; something that is veiled or hidden but suddenly the veil is removed and what was hidden now comes into plain view; because the veil has been removed, what is behind the veil is no longer concealed or hidden from view

19. "confirm" — βεβαιόω (*bebaioo*): to authenticate; to verify; to establish or make concrete
20. "end" — τέλος (*telos*): ripeness, maturity, or completion; the highest point; a climax; a final purpose
21. "blameless" — ἀνέγκλητος (*anegkletos*): unreprovable; irreproachable; unaccused; unable to bring legal charges against; not convictable when closely scrutinized; blameless

SYNOPSIS

In the previous two lessons, we have looked at the Resurrection of Christ Church in Saint Petersburg, Russia — a simply breathtaking church that was officially consecrated in 1907. Its walls are covered with more than 71,000 square feet of mosaics, which were created in a local workshop in the city of Saint Petersburg. And it was built in memory of Alexander II who lost his life on the very ground where the church now stands.

After the communist regime took over Russia, they closed this church in 1930. The enormous bells that hung in the bell tower were melted down, and the plan was to completely demolish the church. But that plan was stopped by the ensuing events of World War II. In fact, during the war, the Resurrection of Christ Church was turned into a morgue. As time passed, it began to be used as a warehouse for potatoes and various types of root vegetables. It was then used as a warehouse for props from a local theater.

Eventually, this once magnificent cathedral fell into complete disrepair and was nearly forgotten for years on end. History records that almost an entire generation of people living in Saint Petersburg never saw the church's exterior — only the rickety scaffolding that shrouded it. But after great effort and persistence, the Resurrection of Christ Church was fully renovated and restored, reopening its doors in 1997 as a museum.

Today it serves as a working church and remains a highly decorated shrine. Along with its 300 mosaics, it also contains special holy gates that lead to the inner chancel of the high altar, and these gates are encrusted with elaborate embellishments. They are truly a treasure. In fact, the whole building is like a treasure.

Yet, as highly decorated as this cathedral is, it pales in comparison to the temple God has made you to be. Second Corinthians 4:7 says, "But we have this treasure in earthen vessels, that the excellency of the power may be of God, and not of us." The word "treasure" in Greek describes something so rich, so immense, and so inexhaustible that it is simply breathtaking.

When God saved you, He placed His greatest treasures inside of you — the riches of Christ. He deposited in you His mercy, His forgiveness, and His love along with His precious blood, the power of His name, and the gifts of His Spirit. You are a living, breathing sanctuary of the Holy Spirit.

The emphasis of this lesson:

The grace of God is His special impartation that enables, empowers, and strengthens the recipients. As the temple of the Holy Spirit, His grace has enriched every area of your life. When God's grace has been liberally poured out, it visibly shows up in the form of the gifts of the Holy Spirit. These gifts of the Spirit authenticate the reality of Jesus.

A Summary of Our Anchor Verse

In First Corinthians 6:19, the apostle Paul wrote to the Corinthian believers who were living way below God's standards and not behaving in the holy way that they should. Out of shock over the reports that had reached his ears, Paul said, "What? know ye not that your body is the temple of the Holy Ghost which is in you, which ye have of God, and ye are not your own?"

We have noted that the first word of this verse — the word "what" — is actually an exclamation. Paul was so stunned by the behavior taking place among believers in Corinth that he began to say, "What! What is this?" He then added the phrase, "Know ye not." In Greek, it is the words *ouk oidate*. The word *ouk* is *an emphatic no*, and the word *oidate* is from the word *oida*, which means *to see, perceive, understand, or comprehend*. When you put all these words together, it is the equivalent of Paul saying, "What's this? Have you not yet understood? Do you really not get it? Have you not realized?"

Even the word "that" is important. It is the Greek word *hoti*, and it points to *the important point* Paul is making. He said, "What? know ye not **that** *your body is the temple of the Holy Ghost...?*" He really wants them to get this point — *that* their body is God's temple. The word "body" is the Greek word *soma*, and it refers to *the physical body*. The fact that your body becomes God's temple is truly a miracle. The moment you surrendered your life to Jesus, God swooped in and transformed your physical body into a divine receptacle or container for the Holy Spirit. You are His temple.

The word "temple" in this verse is the Greek word *naos*, and it describes *a temple* or *a highly decorated shrine*. It is an image of vaulted ceilings, marble, granite, gold, silver, and highly decorated ornamentation. Furthermore, it depicts *the most sacred, innermost part of a temple*; it is the very word used in the Old Testament Septuagint to describe *the Holy of Holies*. And now in this verse, Paul purposely chose the word *naos* to describe what God has transformed us to be — the temple of His Spirit.

If Jesus is your Lord and Savior, then the Holy Spirit has moved inside of you and become a permanent resident in our life. You are now a walking sanctuary. This is what Paul was communicating to the Corinthians, who were behaving in such ungodly ways. He said, "Your body is the temple of the Holy Ghost, which is *in* you."

The word "in" here is significant. It is the Greek word *en*, and it means *in*. It specifically identifies the location of where the Holy Spirit is — *inside* us. Paul then added, "…which ye have of God…" (1 Corinthians 6:19). The words "ye have" is a form of the Greek word *echo*, which means *to have, to hold, to possess*, or *to contain*. Essentially, Paul is saying, "We are the *holders*, the *possessors*, or the *containers* of this amazing temple which we have "of God." The word "of" here is the Greek word *apo*, and it means *directly from God*. The transformation we experienced the day we were saved is not a result of personal rehabilitation or reform. It is something we received directly from God. It is a work of His grace in our lives, and as a result, we are not our own anymore. Our body, soul, and spirit belong to Jesus who loves us and gave Himself for us.

Understanding the Meaning of the Word 'Grace'

As we have seen throughout the previous lessons, our salvation is totally a work of God's grace. Ephesians 2:8 and 9 says, "For by grace are ye saved through faith; and that not of yourselves: it is the gift of God: Not of works, lest any man should boast." Many people today are talking about grace without understanding the historical roots of the word. To better appreciate what God has done in our lives, let's take a look at the origin and meaning of the word "grace."

In the Greek language of the New Testament, the word "grace" is *charis*, and that is the word used in First Corinthians 1:4, which says, "I thank my God always on your behalf, for the *grace* of God which is given you by Jesus Christ." Pages and pages could be written about the origins and the various nuances of meaning contained in this word *charis* — grace. *Charis* denoted *special power that was conferred upon an individual or a group of individuals by the gods.*

Once this *charis* — grace — was conferred upon a person or a group of people, it imparted to them supernatural abilities. In other words, it enabled them to do what they could not normally or naturally do. In some secular literature from the early New Testament period, the word *charis* — this word "grace" — was even used to denote *individuals who had been placed under a magic spell that transformed their personalities and imparted supernatural abilities to them.* All of that is in this word "grace" — the Greek word *charis*.

As used in secular Greek literature, the word *charis* — grace — described a specific moment when an individual experienced a supernatural touch of the gods that always resulted in some type of outward evidence or visible manifestation. In this context, a person or group of people would never experience a supernatural impartation of *charis* without some kind of outward evidence.

In the New Testament, the word "grace" — the same word *charis* — is sometimes translated as the word "favor" because the individual who receives it has been supernaturally enabled as a result of receiving favor from God. So when we read of "grace" in the New Testament, we know it is referring to God graciously imparting a special touch that enables, empowers, and strengthens the recipients. All of this applies to us. We have received a divine touch that has transformed us and given us abilities and graces to do what we could have never done before.

This word "grace" — the Greek word *charis* — describes *those that are enabled, empowered, and strengthened.* It is a touch of God that enhances personalities and imparts to people supernatural abilities, and it is always accompanied by some type of outward evidence or demonstration. Of course it produces inward change, but it always comes with outward evidence. It is never silent, and it is never invisible. It always manifests in some visible, tangible way.

Likewise, if you have been touched by God's grace, you should expect His grace to visibly show up in many areas of your life. His grace will empower you to have victory over sin, and it will enable you to control your tongue. Furthermore, it will transform you as its influence changes your behavior. And by studying this word "grace," particularly in this verse, we find a specific insight regarding this truth. When God's grace has been liberally poured out, it visibly shows up in the form of the gifts of the Holy Spirit.

God's Grace Has Enriched Every Area of Your Life

Turning our attention once more to First Corinthians 1:4, it says, "I thank my God always on your behalf, for the *grace* of God which is given you by Jesus Christ." Again, the word "grace" in this verse is the Greek word *charis*, and it signifies *God's grace that supernaturally equips the recipient*.

In the next verse, Paul went on to say, "That in every thing ye are enriched by him, in all utterance, and in all knowledge" (1 Corinthians 1:5). Notice the words "in every thing." It is a translation of the Greek words *en panti*, which means *in every way* or in *every thing*. It is *an all-encompassing phrase* that means *everything*. Actually, the little word *ti*, which is attached to the word *pan*, describes *every minute and miniscule detail*. If we take this meaning and plug it into this verse, a better translation of it would be, "In everything and in every way — even the most minute, miniscule details of your life — you have been enriched by God's grace."

This brings us to the word "enriched," which is the Greek word *ploutidzo*. It describes *wealth so great it cannot be tabulated*. It is *abundant wealth; vast wealth; extreme riches; incredible abundance; magnificent opulence; and extravagant lavishness*. This word was used by Plato to say no one was richer than the legendary King Midas. Everything he touched seemed to turn to gold. Here, the apostle Paul used the word *ploutidzo* — translated as "enriched" — to describe how God's grace has lavishly adorned us on the inside.

In his very next breath, Paul tells us of a specific area in which we are enriched. He said, "In all utterance." The word "utterance" is a form of the Greek word *logos*, and it means *in all speech*, referring to *the vocal gifts of the*

Holy Spirit. These vocal gifts include specifically *the word of knowledge, the word of wisdom, prophecy, tongues,* and *interpretation of tongues.*

Then Paul adds the phrase "in all knowledge." In Greek, the word "knowledge" is a form of the word *gnosis*, which describes *knowledge.* Specifically, this refers to *the knowledge gifts of the Holy Spirit.* These gifts include *the word of wisdom, the word of knowledge, prophecy,* and *discerning of spirits.* When we look at these knowledge gifts of the Spirit and compare them with the vocal gifts, we can see that there is some overlap between the two.

The Holy Spirit is the possessor of all these gifts and many others, and just as He internally adorned the Corinthian believers with these abilities, He has also adorned you. Again, you are the temple of the Holy Spirit, and all the riches of Christ have been deposited within you. Even if you don't presently see these gifts operating in your life, the potential to manifest and move in these gifts is within you.

The Gifts of the Holy Spirit Authenticate the Reality of Jesus

In First Corinthians 1:6, Paul went on to say, "Even as the testimony of Christ was confirmed in you." The word "testimony" is the Greek word *marturion*, and it describes *a testimony* or *one who gives testimony in a court of law.* The word "confirmed" is a translation of the Greek word *bebaioo*, which means *to authenticate; to verify; to establish or make concrete.* What Paul is saying here is that when the gifts of the Holy Spirit are operating in you, they *establish* and *authenticate* the "testimony of Christ."

Rick shared an example from his life of the importance of the gifts of the Holy Spirit. Throughout his growing years, he had heard many Bible stories of Jesus healing people, but he never actually saw anyone get healed. In his mind, the healing works of Jesus recorded in the gospels were like a fictional fairy tale that happened 2,000 years ago, because he had never seen it happen. However, when he finally saw the gift of healing operate right before his eyes, suddenly, the Jesus of the gospels stepped off the pages and into his life! The Holy Spirit's gift of healing *authenticated* and *verified* the testimony that Jesus Christ is a healer. This is why the gifts of the Holy Spirit are essential. They bring to us the reality of Jesus Christ.

The Gifts of the Holy Spirit Are To Operate in Us Until Christ Returns

Paul continued his discussion with the believers in Corinth, saying, "So that ye come behind in no gift; waiting for the coming of our Lord Jesus Christ (1 Corinthians 1:7). The words "come behind" are a translation of the Greek word *hustereo*, which means *having a lack of sufficiency*. It describes *a deficiency*, *a shortage*, or *a shortfall*. Paul didn't want the Corinthian believers to be lacking or deficient in any spiritual gift as they waited for the "coming" of the Lord.

This word "coming" is the Greek word *apokalupsis*, and it refers to *something that has been veiled or hidden, but then becomes clear and visible to the mind or eye*. It is *an unveiling* or *a sudden revealing*. It means *to uncover*. This word *apokalupsis* — translated here as "coming" — refers to the imminent sudden appearing of Jesus. Although He has been *veiled or hidden from our sight, suddenly the veil will be removed, and He who was hidden will come into plain view*.

In First Corinthians 1:8, Paul described the work of the Holy Spirit as the One "Who shall also confirm you unto the end, that ye may be blameless in the day of our Lord Jesus Christ." The word "confirm" is again the Greek word *bebaioo*, meaning *to authenticate*; *to verify*; *to establish or make concrete*. And the word "end" is the Greek word *telos*, which describes *ripeness, maturity,* or *completion*. It can also indicate *the highest point* or *a climax*; *a final purpose*.

By using these words, Paul is telling us that it is God's intention for the lavish spiritual gifts of the Holy Spirit to operate in us to establish and authenticate who Jesus is, bringing us into full spiritual maturity. In fact, these spiritual gifts are meant to keep us "blameless," which means *unreprovable*; *irreproachable*; *unaccused*. To be "blameless" means *no one is able to bring legal charges against us — we are not convictable when closely scrutinized*.

Friend, your body is the temple of the Holy Spirit! You are a walking sanctuary of God, filled with all the riches of Jesus Christ. You have been bought with a great price — the precious blood of Jesus. In our next lesson, we will look at what it means to be called a "saint" and live a life of holiness.

STUDY QUESTIONS

> Study to shew thyself approved unto God, a workman that needeth not to be ashamed, rightly dividing the word of truth.
> — 2 Timothy 2:15

1. Prior to this lesson, what was your understanding of the *grace* of God? How has this teaching broadened your knowledge and appreciation for His grace?
2. According to James 4:6; First Peter 5:5; and Proverbs 3:34, what must you do — and what is required — for you to receive God's grace? What does the Bible say is the Number 1 obstacle to you receiving His grace?
3. The Bible identifies nine specific *gifts* of the Holy Spirit in First Corinthians 12:8-11 and nine specific *fruits* of the Spirit in Galatians 5:22 and 23. What are these gifts and fruits?
4. Which gifts of the Holy Spirit have you personally seen operating through others? How did the manifestation of those gifts help strengthen your faith? Which gifts of the Holy Spirit have you experienced operating in your life? How have they strengthened the faith of others?

PRACTICAL APPLICATION

> But be ye doers of the word, and not hearers only, deceiving your own selves.
> — James 1:22

1. "Grace" — the Greek word *charis* — describes *those who are enabled, empowered, and strengthened*. It is a touch of God that enhances personalities and imparts to people supernatural abilities, and it is always accompanied by some type of outward evidence or demonstration. What outward evidence in your life can you point to that demonstrates God's grace is on you? What things has He enabled and empowered you to do that you could have never done on your own?
2. As the temple of the Holy Spirit, you are a divine container of God's presence. In His eyes, you are a priceless treasure filled with the fullness of Jesus! Be honest: How do you see yourself — as God's prized possession or a person of little worth? When you make mistakes, do you beat yourself up and put yourself down, or do you readily embrace

God's grace and forgiveness and keep moving forward in faith? If you're struggling to accept God's forgiveness for your failures and His loving approval, pray and ask Him to give you eyes to see yourself the way He sees you.

3. Friend, there are no limits whatsoever to what the grace of God can do. In what areas of your life do you need a tangible manifestation of God's grace? These are areas where you have a tendency to be frustrated, irritated, fearful, or lacking in peace. Take some time to pray and invite the Holy Spirit — who is the "Spirit of grace" (*see* Hebrews 10:29) — into these situations. Ask Him for His grace to see things the way *He* sees them and to do what you need to do to bring Him glory.

LESSON 9

TOPIC

You Are Called To Be a Saint

SCRIPTURES

1. **1 Corinthians 6:19,20** — What? know ye not that your body is the temple of the Holy Ghost which is in you, which ye have of God, and ye are not your own? For ye are bought with a price: therefore glorify God in your body, and in your spirit, which are God's.
2. **Romans 1:7** — To all that be in Rome, beloved of God, called to be saints: Grace to you and peace from God our Father, and the Lord Jesus Christ.
3. **Exodus 3:5** — Draw not nigh hither: put off thy shoes from off thy feet, for the place whereon thou standest is holy ground.

GREEK WORDS

1. "What" — ἤ (*e*): an exclamation
2. "know ye not" — οὐκ οἴδατε (*ouk oidate*): from οὐκ (*ouk*) and οἶδα (*oida*); the word οὐκ (*ouk*) is an emphatic no, and οἶδα (*oida*), to see, perceive, understand, or comprehend; the word οἶδα (*oida*) depicts

knowledge gained by personal experience or personal observation; in this verse, have you not emphatically comprehended

3. "that" — ὅτι (*hoti*): points to an important point
4. "body" — σῶμα (*soma*): the physical body
5. "temple" — ναός (*naos*): a temple or a highly decorated shrine; the image of vaulted ceilings, marble, granite, gold, silver, and highly decorated ornamentation; the most sacred, innermost part of a temple; the holy of holies
6. "in" — ἐν (*en*): literally, in or inside
7. "ye have" — ἔχω (*echo*): to have, hold, or possess
8. "of" — ἀπό (*apo*): from, as directly from God
9. "therefore" — δή (*de*): consequently; subsequently; as a result
10. "glorify" — δοξάζω (*doxadzo*): from δοκέω (*dokeo*), to think or to estimate; honor; value; to show weight and worth
11. "in" — ἐν (*en*): literally, in or inside
12. "saints" — ἅγιος (*hagios*): holy; something that has been separated, consecrated, sanctified, and set apart for special use

SYNOPSIS

The Romanov family, who ruled the Russian Empire, lived in the Winter Palace during winters from 1762 to 1917. Although they had many places to live — including the Peterhof Palace, the Catherine Palace, and the Gatchina Palace — the Winter Palace was their residence during the frigid winter months. It is located in Saint Petersburg, Russia, and although it was designed by Empress Elizabeth, the first person to live in this palace was Catherine the Great.

Inside this magnificent fortress — *its combined floor space on three floors is the equivalent of 12 football fields in size* — is a marvelous church called the Great Church of the Winter Palace. It was designed by Francesco Rastrelli, an Italian architect who has been recognized as the most expensive architect in history. Even today, no architect matches the level of financial fees that Rastrelli could demand. After falling out of favor with Catherine the Great and being dismissed from his post, Rastrelli seems to have suddenly disappeared from history. No one knows exactly what happened to him. Nevertheless, during his life he was magnificently wealthy and designed palaces all over Saint Petersburg and the Russian Empire. And one of his most prized creations was the Great Church of the Winter Palace.

Unfortunately, it fell into disrepair and was closed for many years. But it was eventually renovated and reopened to the public, and today when visitors walk into this church, it nearly takes their breath away. The lavish décor, which includes 11 pounds of gold embellishment on the walls, is quite extraordinary. What is interesting about the Great Church of the Winter Palace is that most of the Romanovs were married there, and those who were had happy marriages and produced many children.

The Great Church of the Winter Palace is a wonderful reminder of the indescribable beauty of God's work in our lives. The moment we said "yes" to Jesus and made Him the Lord of our life, God turned our bodies into the temple of the Holy Spirit. He no longer resides in buildings — He lives in us! And where His *Holy* Spirit lives is *holy* ground. In fact, God calls us His *saints*.

The emphasis of this lesson:

When you surrendered your life to Jesus and His Blood cleansed you and the Holy Spirit moved into your heart, that divine presence consecrated you, separated you, and set you apart for God's special use. You are no longer common or ordinary. Your status has been changed. God has moved you into a new, separate category — the category of a "saint."

A Review of Our Anchor Verse

We have seen that when the apostle Paul wrote to the Corinthian believers in First Corinthians 6:19, he was absolutely stunned by the low-level behavior they were exhibiting. In great shock, he said:

> **What? know ye not that your body is the temple of the Holy Ghost which is in you, which ye have of God, and ye are not your own?**

When you read this passage in the Greek, the word "what" is an exclamation. It is as if Paul is saying, "What! What is this? How is this humanly possible?" He then said, "Know ye not," which in Greek is *ouk oidate* and is a combination of the word *ouk*, which is *an emphatic no*, and a form of the word *oida*, which means *to see, perceive, understand, or comprehend*. When we put these words together, the phrase "What? know ye not" is the equivalent of Paul saying, "What! What are you doing? Do you not yet understand? Have you not really comprehended it?"

Then Paul said, "…**Your body is the temple of the Holy Ghost…**" (1 Corinthians 6:19). The word "body" here is the Greek word *soma*, and it describes the *physical body*. Paul told the Corinthian believers — and us — that our physical body is the temple of the Holy Spirit. The word "temple" is the Greek word *naos*, which is the term for *a temple* or *a highly decorated shrine*. It is the picture of vaulted ceilings, marble, granite, gold, silver, and highly decorated ornamentation. This word *naos* is the same word used in the Old Testament Septuagint to describe *the most sacred, innermost part of a temple*; *the holy of holies*. The Corinthian believers, who were Greek, would have totally understood what Paul was communicating to them here because their cities had numerous temples that were highly decorated shrines.

Paul went on to pinpoint the location — and origin — of this temple by saying, "…[It] is in you, which ye have of God, and ye are not your own?" (1 Corinthians 6:19). The word "in" is the little Greek word *en*, and it identifies that the location of God's temple is *inside* us. If "X" marks the spot of the treasure on the treasure map, then there's a huge "X" on us.

The phrase "which ye have" is a form of the Greek word *echo*, which means *to hold, to have,* or *to possess*. The use of this word here depicts our body as a *divine container* of the presence of Almighty God. Furthermore, the word "of" is the Greek word *apo*, and it means *directly coming from God*. Hence, what happened the day we were saved is not the result of any human effort on our part. The transformation we experienced came *directly from God (apo)*.

Paul concluded First Corinthians 6:19 by saying, "…Ye are not your own," which means we should live with a sense of responsibility and deep gratitude to God for all that He has brought about in our lives. Everything is the result of His divine work of grace, and He is worthy of our praise!

Your Response to God's Great Kindness

In light of all that God has done and the miraculous work that He Himself has brought about in us, the apostle Paul declared in First Corinthians 6:20 what our response should be:

For ye are bought with a price: therefore glorify God in your body, and in your spirit, which are God's.

The word "therefore" is the Greek word *de*, which means *consequently*, *subsequently*, or *as a result*. Basically, Paul said, "As a result of and in response to what Jesus did, glorify God in your body and in your spirit."

The word "glorify" is the Greek word *doxadzo*. It is a form of the word *dokeo*, which means *to think* or *to estimate*. The use of this word tells us that in order to glorify God, we really need to *put our minds to it*. We can't be halfhearted about it or just hope it happens. The word *dokeo* — translated here as "glorify" — means we are to strongly consider the value, the weight, and the worth of how we can best bring God glory.

Now, when many believers hear, "…Therefore glorify God in your body, and in your spirit…" (1 Corinthians 6:20), they think, *Well, I'm already glorifying God in my spirit because that is where He lives*. Although this is true, the verse also says you are to glorify Him in your "body." Here again is the Greek word *soma*, which describes *the physical human body*. When Jesus died, He not only redeemed your spirit, He also redeemed your body. Therefore, it is no longer yours but His, and He wants you to make a well thought-out decision of how you can best glorify Him with it. Remember, your body is the temple of the Holy Spirit.

You Have Been Separated, Consecrated, and Sanctified for God's Special Use

Since you are a walking sanctuary of the Holy Spirit, God has internally decorated you with holiness. In fact, He calls you a "saint." Paul made this distinction in Romans 1:7 when he opened his letter to the believers who were in Rome. He said, "To all that be in Rome, beloved of God, called to be saints: Grace to you and peace from God our Father, and the Lord Jesus Christ."

Notice that word "saints." It is a form of the Greek word *hagios*, which means *holy*. It describes *something that has been separated, consecrated, sanctified and set apart for special use*. The interesting thing about this word *hagios* is that it depicts *something that was once very common and very natural, but something has suddenly happened to it to change its status*. It is no longer common, ordinary, or natural; it has become *hagios* — it is *separated, consecrated, and sanctified as holy*. It will never again be regarded in a common way. It is so different it has been moved into a category of its own. All of this meaning is found in the Greek word *hagios*, which is translated here as "saints."

There are actually multiple places in the New Testament where Christians are called "saints" (*hagios*). These include: Romans 1:7; 1 Corinthians 6:1 and 16:1; 2 Corinthians 9:1; Ephesians 5:3; Colossians 1:4, 1:12, 1:26; Philippians 1:1 and 4:21,22; 1 Thessalonians 3:13; 2 Thessalonians 1:10; Philemon 1:5 and 1:7; Hebrews 13:24; and Revelations 17:6.

Friend, once you call upon Jesus and receive Him as your Lord and Savior, you are no longer who you used to be. Your status has changed. God has moved you into a separate category — the category of a "saint."

The First Use of the Word 'Holy' in Scripture

Let's journey backward in time to a moment recorded in Exodus 3:5 where the word "holy" was first used. Moses had renounced his position as the son of Pharaoh's daughter and had become a shepherd in the wilderness of Sinai. The Bible tells us that one day as he was tending his sheep on the backside of Mount Horeb, he saw a burning bush that was not consumed by the fire.

Moses turned to see this astounding phenomenon. Scripture says he saw it as a "great sight" — something that stunned and amazed him, for he had never witnessed anything like it. When Moses drew near, the voice of God called out to him from the midst of the burning bush and said, "…Draw not nigh hither: put off thy shoes from off thy feet, for the place whereon thou standest is holy ground" (Exodus 3:5).

In that hallowed moment, Moses crossed the threshold that separated the natural realm from the realm that God called "holy." The physical location that Moses entered at that moment was so sacred to God that He commanded him to remove his shoes, lest Moses carry the contamination of the dirt on him unto that holy spot of earth that had become God's sanctuary.

The word "holy" in Exodus 3:5 is *hagia* in the Old Testament Greek Septuagint. It is a translation of the Greek word *hagios* and is used here for the first time in Scripture to describe the sudden transformation that occurred when God's presence touched that place and forever changed its status. From this point forward throughout the Bible, this is the word used to denote the holiness of God, the holy presence of God, or anything that God deems to be holy.

Mount Horeb Became Known As The 'Holy' Mount

If you were able to travel back in time to the Sinai Peninsula and see Mount Horeb during Moses' day, it wouldn't have looked any different than the other surrounding mountains. There was nothing particularly unique about that mountain in terms of its appearance compared to other mountains. But God's presence had touched it, and in that moment, His divine presence supernaturally separated Mount Horeb from all other mountains and set it apart into a holy category.

When Moses approached the burning bush, God told him to remove his shoes because he was standing on "holy" ground. Because that word "holy" in this context is a form of the Greek word *hagios*, it tells us God consecrated and sanctified that mountain. It became so sacred at that moment that it grew to be known as the *Holy Mount*. Although it was nestled in the midst of an entire mountain range of normal mountains, on that day, Horeb ceased to be normal from that moment forward. God's presence had changed its status.

That is what happens when God's Presence touches something. It consecrates it, sanctifies it, and puts it into a new category. That is what the word "holy" means and why Mount Horeb is called the *Holy Mount* to this day. It was just a mountain, until God's presence touched it. And when God's presence touched it, everything about that mountain was changed.

God's Word Is Called the 'Holy' Bible

Another example of the word "holy" is found in the name given to the Scriptures. The King James translators were some of the earliest to give the Bible's full name as the *Holy Bible*. The word "Bible" is in reality a translation of the Greek word *biblios*, which simply means *book* or *a scroll of writing*. And the word "holy" — the Greek word *hagios* — means *separated, consecrated, holy,* or *sacred*. It describes *something that is never to be regarded or used in a common way*.

Anything that is "holy" is in a category that is *separate* and *sacred* from other things. That means the *Holy Bible* is a special book that is *consecrated*, *separated*, and *set apart* from all other books. Although it may look like an ordinary book, the *Holy Bible* is like no other. If you walk into a library, you will find a copy of the *Holy Bible* on its shelves. Even though it is located in a library full of books, the word "holy" in the name *Holy Bible* signifies that it is in a category all by itself.

And every time you call that precious Book by its name — *Holy Bible* — you are affirming that it is like no other book. You are declaring it is *set apart* into a *special, consecrated, holy* category, and that it is different from all the other books in the library. The *Holy Bible* is so different that no other book in the world that has ever been written compares to it.

So we've seen that God's Word is in a category all by itself because it is the *Holy Bible*. We've also seen that Mount Horeb is in a category all by itself because it is the *Holy Mount*. Again, the word "holy" is the Greek word *hagios*, which describes *something that is separate, sacred, consecrated, and holy*. It is not common or ordinary; it is in a divine category by itself. This word *hagios* — the Greek word for "holy" — is the same word translated as "saint" or "saints" throughout the Scriptures. Let's take a look at how Paul used this word *hagios* in the New Testament as the word "saints."

All Believers Are God's 'Saints'

When Paul wrote to the Christians in Rome — as well as to all believers everywhere — he began his letter by saying, "To all that be in Rome, beloved of God, called to be *saints*..." (Romans 1:7).

Sometimes when people see the word "saints," they imagine individuals with halos above their heads. But that is not what this means. The word translated "saints" here is actually a form of the Greek word *hagios* — the same word we have been studying throughout this lesson. It describes something that has been *separated, consecrated, sanctified*, and *set apart* for special use.

Before we became Christians, we were common, ordinary human beings just like everyone else. But when we surrendered our lives to Jesus and His blood cleansed us and the Holy Spirit moved into our hearts, that divine presence *consecrated us, set us apart*, and made us so *different* that God immediately saw us in a special, holy light that was different from unsaved people. We are now in an entirely new category that He calls "holy" — *hagios*.

So when Paul called the Christians in Rome (and you and me) "saints," he was really saying that *we are called to be holy, called to be different, called to be sanctified,* or *called to be separate from the rest of the world.* In a fraction of a split second, quicker than the mind can comprehend, the Holy Spirit's presence within us, removed us from the category of normal human beings and moved us over into the special category of *set-apart, consecrated, marked-off, holy beings,* created in God's own image.

That is what the word "saints" means to you and me. This means that if you are a believer, you may look like any other human being in society, but you are not like everyone else. God Himself is living on the inside of you!

Just as the presence of God came down on Mount Horeb and made it holy, and just as the Holy Bible is sacred and different than every other book, the moment the blood of Jesus washed you and the Holy Spirit entered your spirit, God *separated* you, *consecrated* you, and *set you apart* for Himself. Friend, you are the forever home of the Holy Spirit — and as such, you are *holy*.

God justified us and made us to be righteous by faith — and in that act, we moved over into a new category of human beings! We might look like regular people, but there is *nothing* regular about us. As new creations who are separated into a higher, holy category, God expects us to adjust our thinking and behave accordingly.

We should no longer think and act as we once did, because we are not who we once were. We are new, different, and holy — and that means we must think differently, talk differently, and act differently. God's Spirit inside us has permanently changed our status! We are the temple of the Holy Spirit.

In our final lesson, we will examine the amazing blessing of being represented by a personal High Priest, Jesus Christ.

STUDY QUESTIONS

> **Study to shew thyself approved unto God, a workman that needeth not to be ashamed, rightly dividing the word of truth.**
> **— 2 Timothy 2:15**

When Moses heard God's voice and approached the burning bush, he stepped onto holy ground and into the very presence of God. It is important for you to know what the Bible says about you entering God's holy presence.

1. By what authority can you enter God's presence?
   (*Read* Hebrews 10:19-22 and First Peter 1:18,19; as well as John 14:6 and Ephesians 2:18.)
2. What does God require before entering His presence? What do you think this means in practical terms? (*See* Psalm 15:1-5 and 24:3-5; Matthew 5:8; Romans 5:1,2.)
3. What should be your attitude when you enter God's presence?
   (*Read* Ephesians 3:12 and Hebrews 4:14-16.)

PRACTICAL APPLICATION

> But be ye doers of the word, and not hearers only, deceiving your own selves.
> —James 1:22

To get an honest appraisal of your status as one of God's "saints," take a few moments to honestly evaluate how you are treating the temple of the Holy Spirit.

1. What are you putting into your temple? Are you eating and drinking healthy things, or do you not really care about what you consume?
2. What kind of shape is your temple in? Are you exercising and doing what you can to stay physically fit, or have you neglected your body and let it fall into disrepair?
3. What is the condition of your *soul*? What are you taking in through your eyes and ears on a regular basis, and how is it affecting the way you think, the way you feel, and the decisions you make?
4. Take a moment to look back on your answers to the above questions. If you realize you have not done your best, don't feel guilty or condemned. Simply repent of any wrongdoing and receive His forgiveness (*see* 1 John 1:9).
5. What practical steps can you take in these areas to begin caring for your temple the way God wants you to? Write down any specific actions you sense Him prompting you to take, and ask Him for the grace to carry them out.

LESSON 10

TOPIC

You Are Represented by a Personal High Priest

SCRIPTURES

1. **1 Corinthians 6:19** — What? know ye not that your body is the temple of the Holy Ghost which is in you, which ye have of God, and ye are not your own?
2. **Romans 1:7** — To all that be in Rome, beloved of God, called to be saints: Grace to you and peace from God our Father, and the Lord Jesus Christ.
3. **Exodus 3:5** — Draw not nigh hither: put off thy shoes from off thy feet, for the place whereon thou standest is holy ground.
4. **Hebrews 4:14-16** — Seeing then that we have a great high priest, that is passed into the heavens, Jesus the Son of God, let us hold fast our profession. For we have not an high priest which cannot be touched with the feeling of our infirmities; but was in all points tempted like as we are, yet without sin. Let us therefore come boldly unto the throne of grace, that we may obtain mercy, and find grace to help in time of need.

GREEK WORDS

1. "What" — ἤ (*e*): an exclamation
2. "know ye not" — οὐκ οἴδατε (*ouk oidate*): from οὐκ (*ouk*) and οἶδα (*oida*); the word οὐκ (*ouk*) is an emphatic no, and οἶδα (*oida*), to see, perceive, understand, or comprehend; the word οἶδα (*oida*) depicts knowledge gained by personal experience or personal observation; in this verse, have you not emphatically comprehended
3. "that" — ὅτι (*hoti*): points to an important point
4. "body" — σῶμα (*soma*): the physical body
5. "temple" — ναός (*naos*): a temple or a highly decorated shrine; the image of vaulted ceilings, marble, granite, gold, silver, and highly dec-

orated ornamentation; the most sacred, innermost part of a temple; the holy of holies

6. "in" — ἐν (*en*): literally, in or inside
7. "ye have" — ἔχω (*echo*): to have, hold, or possess
8. "of" — ἀπό (*apo*): from, as directly from God
9. "hold fast" — κρατέω (*krateo*): power; to seize, to take hold of, to firmly grip, or to apprehend; denotes strength, power, victory over something, taking something by force, or storming something; the idea of making a forceful arrest; to have power over, to hold fast to, or to have a masterful grip on
10. "touched" — συμπαθέω (*sumpatheo*): to sympathize; to feel what another feels
11. "tempted" — πειράζω (*peiradzo*): temptation; an intense examination done to prove the fitness of an object; an outside pressure or source that appeals to one's weakness; a temptation to affect one mentally, emotionally, or sensually; can describe any weakness of the flesh
12. "like" — ὁμοιότης (*homoiotes*): similarly; in like manner
13. "without" — χωρὶς (*choris*): to be outside of something, such as someone who lives outside the perimeters of a city; a comparison between being outside or inside something; depicts someone who is out of, not in, a specific location; to be separate, to be without, to have nothing to do with
14. "sin" — ἁμαρτία (*hamartia*): to miss the mark; a failure; a fault
15. "boldly" — παρρησία (*parresia*): a bold, frank, forthright speech; confidence; audacious; emboldened; openness; extraordinarily frank; boldness; assurance; unashamed confidence
16. "throne" — θρόνος (*thronos*): throne or the highest seat of power
17. "grace" — χάρις (*charis*): a touch of the gods resulting in favor or grace; an empowering touch; an empowering presence, always demonstrating itself with a visible manifestation; a power that changes individuals; a power that enables one to do what he previously could not do or to be what he could never previously be
18. "obtain" — λαμβάνω (*lambano*): to seize or to lay hold of something in order to make it your very own, almost like a person who reaches out to grab, to capture, or to take possession of something; in some cases, it means to violently lay hold of something in order to seize and

take it as one's very own; at other times it depicts one who graciously receives something that is freely and easily given

19. "mercy" — ἔλεος (*eleos*): pity; emotion that compels one to action
20. "find" — εὑρίσκω (*heurisko*): to find or to discover; a discovery made as a result of serious searching; points to a discovery made due to an intense investigation, scientific study, or scholarly research
21. "grace" — χάρις (*charis*): a touch of the gods resulting in favor or grace; an empowering touch; an empowering presence, always demonstrating itself with a visible manifestation; a power that changes individuals; a power that enables one to do what he previously could not do or to be what he could never previously be
22. "help" — βοήθεια (*boetheia*): to help; first and foremost a military term to depict the moment when a soldier heard that his fellow fighter was entrenched in battle, captured, or struggling, and who once alerted to this situation, that nearby soldier quickly went into action to fight for the safety and well-being of his fellow fighter; the fellow soldier spared no effort to deliver his comrade and urgently acted to rescue and bring him back into a place of safety, security, and protection

SYNOPSIS

Inside the magnificent Winter Palace in Saint Petersburg, Russia, is a marvelous church called the Great Church of the Winter Palace. It was designed by the famous Italian architect Francesco Rastrelli. Over time, the church fell into disrepair and was closed for many years. Eventually it was renovated and reopened to the public, and today when visitors walk into this church, they are simply in awe of its beauty. The extravagant décor on the walls includes 11 pounds of gold ornamentation, and it is breathtaking to behold!

It was in this church that many members of the Romanov family were wedded and went on to enjoy happy marriages and produce many children. It was also in this church that Nicholas II, who was the last tsar of Russia, came to pray before he walked onto the balcony of the Hermitage to publicly announce that he was declaring war with Germany in 1914.

What is interesting to note is that today there is actually a priest who serves and conducts services in the Great Church of the Winter Palace. It reminds us of the fact that as believers, we too have a Priest, and His name is Jesus. And we are the marvelous temple of the Holy Spirit. Although our interiors are not covered with costly gold or silver, we are filled with something much more valuable — the presence of God Himself.

Since the day we surrendered our lives to Him and He took up permanent residence inside of us by the power of His Holy Spirit, Jesus has served as our great High Priest and continues to pray and intercede for us continually. If we will just come to God's throne of grace, He is willing and ready to help us in our time of need.

The emphasis of this lesson:

Jesus is your personal High Priest. He was tempted in every way that you are, yet He never entered into sin. God wants you to come boldly before His throne and receive His grace and mercy. Jesus is ready to swing into action and give you the help you need when you need it.

In the past nine lessons, we have unearthed truths from several New Testament passages to better understand what it means to be the temple of the Holy Spirit.

- In **Lesson 1**, we studied Ephesians 2:1-5 and learned that *you are God's special project*.
- In **Lesson 2**, we analyzed Ephesians 2:10 and saw that *you are God's masterpiece*, created brand-spanking new in Christ Jesus.
- In **Lesson 3**, we examined John 1:12 and discovered that *you have been born by the power of God* and have been given the legal right to become His son or daughter.
- In **Lesson 4**, we found out that when God finished His transforming work, *you were sealed with the Holy Spirit* who also serves as a down payment or guarantee of your full redemption.
- In **Lesson 5**, we dissected the meaning of Second Corinthians 4:7, which says *you are a repository of God's greatest treasure* — the gift of the Holy Spirit.
- In **Lesson 6**, we focused on Second Corinthians 5:17 and what it means to be *a brand-new creature in Christ*. You are not a reformed or rehabilitated version of what you used to be; you are brand-spanking new, which required a great deal of power to accomplish.

- In **Lesson 7**, we explored First Corinthians 3:16, which tells us that *you are part of the corporate temple of the Holy Spirit.*
- In **Lesson 8**, we learned what it means to be *filled with the riches of Christ.*
- And in **Lesson 9**, we reflected on Romans 1:7 and discovered that *God has called you to be a saint.*

A Final Review of Our Anchor Verse

In First Corinthians 6:19, Paul wrote to the believers in Corinth and said, "What? know ye not that your body is the temple of the Holy Ghost which is in you, which ye have of God, and ye are not your own?"

As we have seen, the believers in Corinth were involved in activities that were far below God's standards. They were getting drunk, going to see prostitutes, and falling back into previous sinful behaviors that were not fitting for a follower of Christ. Paul's shock over their behavior is seen in the opening word of this verse — the word "what," which in Greek is an exclamation. It's the equivalent of Paul saying, "What! What is this?" Then he said, "Know ye not," which in Greek is *ouk oidate*. It is taken from the word *ouk*, which is *an emphatic no*, and the word *oida*, which means *to see, perceive, understand, or comprehend.* When we put these words together, the phrase "What? know ye not" is the equivalent of Paul saying, "What! What are you doing? Do you not yet understand? Have you not yet gotten it?"

Then he said, "…That your body is the temple of the Holy Ghost?" (1 Corinthians 6:19). The Greek word for "body" here is *soma*, and it denotes *the physical body.* The moment you were saved, God miraculously transformed your physical body into a "temple" for His Spirit to live in. We have seen that the word "temple" here is the Greek word *naos*, which describes *a temple or a highly decorated shrine.* It is the picture of vaulted ceilings and marble columns along with granite, gold, silver, and highly decorated ornamentation. It is actually the same word used in the Old Testament Septuagint to describe *the innermost part of the temple in Jerusalem* or *the Holy of Holies.*

Paul knew what the word *naos* meant when he used it and so did his readers. It was as if he was saying, "If your eyes were opened and you could observe your spiritual interiors, you would be absolutely stunned by what you'd see. Inwardly, you have been lavishly decorated with the power of

God, the gifts of the Holy Spirit, the matchless blood of Jesus, and the very character of God Himself. You are a walking sanctuary of God's Spirit!"

Paul went on to reveal that the location — and source — of the temple "…is in you, which ye have of God…" (1 Corinthians 6:19). The word "in" is the Greek word *en*, and it tells us that the location of God's temple is *inside* you. If "X" marks the spot of the treasure on the treasure map, then there's a huge "X" on you.

The phrase "which ye have" is a form of the Greek word *echo*, which means *to hold, to have,* or *to possess*. The use of this word here depicts your body as *a divine container* of God's presence. Furthermore, the word "of" is the Greek word *apo*, and it means *directly coming from God*. Hence, what happened the day you were saved is not the result of any human effort on your part. The transformation you experienced came *directly from God* (*apo*).

Paul ended First Corinthians 6:19 by saying, "…Ye are not your own," which means you should live with a sense of responsibility and sincere appreciation to God for all that He has produced in your life. It is by His grace and His grace alone that you are who you are, and He deserves your very best!

Jesus Is Your Personal High Priest

In Hebrews 4:14, the Bible says, "Seeing then that we have a great high priest, that is passed into the heavens, Jesus the Son of God, let us hold fast our profession." In New Testament times, every temple had a high priest. And since we are the temple of the Holy Spirit, we have a high priest too. His name is Jesus.

When the Bible says, "…Let us hold fast our profession," the words "hold fast" are a translation of the Greek word *krateo*, which describes *power*. It means *to seize, to take hold of, to firmly grip, or to apprehend*. It denotes *strength, power, or victory over something*. It depicts *taking something by force*, or *storming something*. It is the idea of *making a forceful arrest*. It can also mean *to have power over something, to hold fast to something*, or *to have a masterful grip on something*. Because you have a great high priest in Jesus, God is urging you to *seize* and *get a victorious grip on* your profession of faith.

Jesus Knows What It's Like To Be Assaulted by Temptation

The writer of Hebrews goes on to say, "For we have not an high priest which cannot be touched with the feeling of our infirmities…" (Hebrews 4:15). The word "touched" here is the Greek word *sumpatheo*. It is a compound of the word *sum*, which describes *something that is equally shared*, and the word *patheo*, which means *to sympathize* or *to feel what another feels*. Jesus can personally sympathize with whatever you're going through, because He has felt it Himself.

Specifically, the Bible says that Jesus, "…was in all points tempted like as we are, yet without sin" (Hebrews 4:15). The word "tempted" here is the Greek word *peiradzo*, which describes *temptation*. But this isn't just any temptation. It is *an intense examination done to prove the fitness of an object*. This word depicts *an outside pressure or source that appeals to one's weakness*. It is *a temptation to affect one mentally, emotionally, or sensually*, and it can describe *any weakness of the flesh*.

According to this verse, Jesus experienced times of intense examination to prove His character. He felt outside pressures and temptations that affected Him mentally, emotionally, and physically. For instance, we know from Luke's gospel that Jesus experienced such intense emotional and mental anguish in the Garden of Gethsemane that many of the capillaries in His body burst, and He sweat drops of blood (*see* Luke 22:44).

But Jesus Never Entered Into Sin

Indeed, He was in all points tempted "…like as we are, yet without sin" (Hebrews 4:15). The word "like" is the Greek word *homoiotes*, which means *similarly* or *in like manner*. Thus, Jesus faced the same types of tests and temptations that we face, yet He was "without sin." In Greek, the word "without" is the word *choris*, which means *to be outside of something, such as someone who lives outside the perimeters of a city*. It depicts *someone who is out of, not in, a specific location*. It means *to be separate, to be without, to have nothing to do with*.

Even though Jesus was severely tempted and placed under intense examination, He stood on the outside of sin and never had anything to do with it. The word "sin" in this verse is the Greek word *hamartia*, which means *to miss the mark*. It carries the idea of *a personal failure* or *a fault*. Despite the fact that Jesus suffered extreme pressures, He held on to His profession of faith and never experienced personal failure. And because of what He endured, He is able to sympathize with you as He serves as your High Priest.

Come Boldly Before God's Throne

In Hebrews 4:16, the Bible says, "Let us therefore come boldly unto the throne of grace, that we may obtain mercy, and find grace to help in time of need." Notice God instructs us to "come boldly unto the throne." The word "boldly" is the Greek word *parresia*, and it describes *a bold, frank, forthright speech* or *confidence*. It depicts *one that is audacious* or *emboldened*. It can also denote an *openness, boldness, assurance,* or *unashamed confidence*. The use of this word clearly tells us that God wants us to approach Him unashamedly and boldly ask Him for help.

And He wants us to come to His "throne." This is the Greek word *thronos*, which describes *a throne* or *the highest seat of power*. The earliest use of *thronos* described physical chairs in people's homes that were reserved solely for the head of a household — perhaps at the family dinner table. In ancient times, the man of the house held supreme authority over all domestic matters, and he had the final say-so in all decisions or business transactions that might affect his family.

Thus, the word *thronos* — translated here as "throne" — denotes the seat of the undisputed master of a house. He has the final say-so in all decisions and all transactions. This is the word the writer of Hebrews chose to use to describe the level of God's authority. Just as the head of a household was the undisputed master of his house, Jesus is the uncontested highest power of the universe. There is no higher authority, law, or power than King Jesus! And we have the privilege of coming right before His throne, which is called the "throne of grace."

Receive God's Grace and Obtain His Mercy

The word "grace" in Hebrews 4:16 is the Greek word *charis*, which is the same word we saw in First Corinthians 1:4 (*see* Lesson 8). The earliest use of the word *charis* described *a touch of the gods resulting in favor or grace*. For you as a believer, it depicts *an empowering touch* or *an empowering presence, always demonstrating itself with a visible, supernatural manifestation*. It is *a power that changes individuals; a power that enables one to do what he previously could not do or to be what he could never previously be.*

God invites you to come boldly and unashamedly before His throne to ask for His supernatural, empowering touch that you need to get through the difficult challenges you are facing. He also wants you to "obtain mercy." The word "obtain" is the Greek word *lambano*, which means *to seize or to lay hold of something in order to make it your very own*, almost like a person who reaches out to grab, to capture, or to take possession of something. In some cases, it means *to violently lay hold of something in order to seize and take it as one's very own*. At other times it depicts *one who graciously receives something that is freely and easily given*.

When you come to God's throne, He freely offers you the divine empowerment of His grace, but you have to reach out in faith and take hold of it and make it your very own. He also offers you "mercy," which is a translation of the Greek word *eleos*, and it describes *pity* or *compassion*. It is *an emotion that compels one to action*.

The Bible says if you will boldly and fearlessly come before God's throne, you will "…obtain mercy, and find grace to help in time of need" (Hebrews 4:16). The word "find" here is the Greek word *heurisko*, which means *to find or to discover*. It is *a discovery made as a result of serious searching*. Specifically, it points to *a discovery made due to an intense investigation, scientific study, or scholarly research*. The word *heurisko* — translated here as "find" — is where we get the word *eureka*. Thus, when you come boldly before God's throne and unashamedly ask for His grace and mercy, you will experience a *eureka* moment. You will find the "help" you need exactly when you need it.

Jesus Will Give You the Help You Need When You Need It

This brings us to the word "help," which is the Greek word *boetheia*. First and foremost it is *a military term to depict the moment when a soldier heard that his fellow fighter was entrenched in battle, captured, or struggling, and who once alerted to this situation, that nearby soldier quickly went into action to fight for the safety and well-being of his fellow fighter*. The fellow soldier spared no effort to deliver his comrade and urgently acted to rescue and bring him back into a place of safety, security, and protection.

Friend, Jesus is your fellow soldier fighting right alongside you against the forces of evil. If you will come boldly to the throne of God's grace, He will hear your cries for help and *quickly move into action to fight for your safety and well-being*. He will spare no effort to deliver you, his fellow comrade, and urgently act to rescue and bring you back into a place of safety, security, and protection.

Jesus is waiting to hear from you! You are the temple of the Holy Spirit, and He is your personal High Priest. Be audacious and come boldly before God's throne, and you will receive His grace — His empowering, supernatural presence that enables you to do what you could never do on your own. Jesus fully understands the stress and the strain of being tempted and tested by the enemy. He was intensely examined just as you are, yet He did not enter into sin. In His mercy, He will have compassion on you and be compelled to act on your behalf.

STUDY QUESTIONS

> **Study to shew thyself approved unto God, a workman that needeth not to be ashamed, rightly dividing the word of truth.**
> **— 2 Timothy 2:15**

1. The apostle John described Jesus as the Word and said, "…Christ became a human being and lived here on earth among us…" (John 1:14 *TLB*). Why was it crucial for Jesus to literally become flesh and blood like us? Take a few moments to reflect on Hebrews 2:14-18 and 4:14-16 and identify the purpose of this in your own words.
2. Proverbs 28:1 says that the righteous are *bold as a lion*. Right now you may not feel very bold, but there is a way you can receive boldness — it is the same way the disciples did in Acts 4:23-31. Read this passage and identify your source of boldness. (*Also consider* Acts 4:13; Isaiah 12:2; Hebrews 13:5,6; Jude 20.)
3. When you boldly come before God's throne, one of the things He offers you is His *mercy*. In your own words, describe what you understand God's mercy to be. What amazing promise does the prophet Jeremiah give in Lamentations 3:22 and 23 about God's mercy? How grateful are you for His mercy?

PRACTICAL APPLICATION

> But be ye doers of the word, and not hearers only,
> deceiving your own selves.
> —James 1:22

Hebrews 4:16 says that if you boldly come before God's throne, you will "...obtain mercy, and find grace to help in time of need." Take a few moments to think back on a very intense time of testing you faced and how you sought God in prayer and experienced a genuine *eureka* moment when you received God's grace.

1. How did God's supernatural empowerment visibly manifest in your life and situation?
2. What did His grace help you do that you could have never done on your own?
3. What overwhelming challenge are you facing right now? Describe it.
4. How does the memory of God's empowerment in the past encourage you to boldly approach His throne now for help in your current situation?

www.ingramcontent.com/pod-product-compliance
Lightning Source LLC
Chambersburg PA
CBHW060408050426
42449CB00009B/1932